The Kangaroo Factor

Dream Big! Think Big!
Seize The Moment!

Other Books By Stephen M. Gower, CSP

What Do They See When They See You Coming?
The Power of Perception Over Reality

Think Like A Giraffe
A Reach For The Sky Guide In Creativity And Maximum Performance

Advocacy Required
Transform Your Customer Into Your #1 Sales Ally

Upsize Selling
Increase Your Sales With The Mix Of Six

Like A Pelican In The Desert
Leadership Redefined: Beyond Awkwardness

Zebra Dazzle
How To Build Stunning Teams

Have You Encouraged Someone Today?
366 Ways To Practice Encouragement

Celebrate The Butterflies
Presenting With Confidence In Public

The Art Of Killing Kudzu
Management By Encouragement

The Missing Lynx
Public Speaking For High School Students

The Focus Crisis
Nurturing Focus Within A Culture Of Change

The Kangaroo Factor

Dream Big! Think Big! Seize The Moment!

A Guide for Leaving
Your Postponement
Pouch And Leaping
Toward Your Dream

Stephen M. Gower

Certified Speaking Professional

Lectern Publishing
P.O. Box 1065, Toccoa, GA 30577

THE KANGAROO FACTOR – Dream Big! Think Big! Seize The Moment! Copyright © 2000 by Stephen M. Gower. All Rights Reserved.

No part of this book may be reproduced, stored, or transmitted in any form or by any electronic or mechanical means including photocopying, recording, information storage and retrieval systems, or otherwise, without written permission from Stephen M. Gower.

First edition, published 2000 by LECTERN PUBLISHING, P. O. Box 1065, Toccoa, GA 30577

Although the author has exhaustively researched all sources to ensure the accuracy and completeness of the information contained in this book, we assume no responsibility for errors, omissions, inaccuracies, or any other inconsistency herein. Any slights or mistakes are purely unintentional.

Library of Congress Catalog Card No.: 99-95252
ISBN: 1-880150-99-9

Dedicated To Phil

When he reads this dedication, he will notice for the first time what I have known for quite a while. Phil Parker will be surprised. No, he will be stunned. Phil will call from Atlanta with an emotional twinge touching his voice. He will ask, "Gower, what in the world were you thinking?" I will respond, "Phil, it was easy and so very natural. I am glad you were pleasantly surprised. After all, serendipity is at the heart of our friendship."

For several years I have been the beneficiary of a remarkable relationship with a fellow speaker and author who perpetually catches me by surprise. The fact that our friendship could intensify so quickly is a bonus gift for both of us as we approach our real "learning years."

I dedicate this book to my friend Phil Parker because he is my encouragement-buddy. He incessantly challenges me to Dream Big, Think Big, and Seize My Opportunity-Moments. Thank you, Phil.

Contents

An Introduction 9

Choose Your City
I.   Where Do You Want To Live? 25
II.   Why Would You Choose Could City? 39
III. Have You Thought About Do City? 43

Delight In Your Dream
IV.   Give Your Dream A Name 51
V.   Give Your Dream A Wake-Up Call 61
VI. Give In To Joy 69

Target Your Thoughts
VII.   Think About The Thoughts You Think 105
VIII. Tell Your Past Where To Go 117
IX.   Throw Your Negative Thoughts In The Dump . 133
X.   Take Your Positive Thoughts To The Bank 153

Seize Your Moments
XI.   Empty Or Full? 173
XII. Mystery, Misery, Or Mastery? 197

Celebrate The Cycle
XIII. A Higher Consciousness 245
XIV. The Discipline Of Mastery 251
XV. A Treasury Of Power Points 253

An Introduction

rob • ber (rob'ər), n.: see self

Who steals your best from you? Who takes the smile out of your spirit? Who siphons the bounce out of your new beginnings? Who robs you of direction, discipline, and delight? Who dwarfs your dreams, tarnishes your thoughts, impedes your initiatives? Who swindles your capacity to leap and keeps you pinned in your postponement-pouch? Who keeps your dreams from equaling reality?

Enough. The answer is simple . . . frightfully so. The thief does not equal "them." It does not

THE KANGAROO FACTOR

equal "it." Ultimately, others cannot abscond with your excitement – unless you cooperate with them. The rudder of your life cannot be embezzled by events – unless you fully cooperate with these events. Nothing can swindle your dreams – unless you allow it to happen. There is not a bandit out there who can rob you of your robust responsibility to be yourself – unless you allow it to happen. There is no con man out there who can get at the core of your spirit – unless you agree to the intrusion. Ultimately, nothing can happen to defraud you of personal growth – unless you give into the thievery. Events will never deprive you of your spunk, your savvy, your spirit – unless you say "yes" to them.

    Oh, for sure, there will be deterrents and detours. But domination of the essence of your spirit? No way – unless you give your consent. Ultimately, the one who cheats you of your greatness is not named Dad or Department Head, Mom or Magistrate, Downline or Upline, God or Government, Coach or Comrade, Teacher or Traffic Cop. In the final analysis, that which swipes away, or pilfers, your maximum performance is not named Cancellation or Confusion, Tax Time or Traffic Trauma, Stock Slide or Summer Sizzle, Merger or Meddling, Finals or even Fatigue!

An Introduction

· Again, enough! You know who the robber is! You know who is swindler-supreme when it comes to ultimate deception. You and I must take responsibility for our own smallness. We counterfeit ourselves when we press the shift-the-blame button. We cheat ourselves when we incessantly rationalize away our responsibility for our own predicament. Rarely do we choose to soar. Seldom do we see ourselves as the sludge that keeps us down.

This book shouts, "Stop your perpetual rationalizing." It yells, "It does not have to stay like it is!" It screams, "You do not have to stay the way you are!" It bellows, "Just as the kangaroo leaps, so can you leap from where you are to where you want to be."

You can overcome adversity and leave your "as-is" in the dust. You need not succumb to others or obstacles or "overwhelmment." You can recognize your capacity to quick-start yourself. You can cease the rationalizing. You can release your marvelous potential for excellence. You can transcend success and touch your own ultimate "soaring." You can leave your "postponement-pouch," that kangaroo-like place that has held your reluctance for far too long. And, in kangaroo-style, you can leap toward bigness! You can enjoy both the leaping and the landing!

THE KANGAROO FACTOR

However, you may be standing in your own way. The resulting blockage will choke away your best breath, your wisest decisions, your smartest moves. You need to do something about the blockage. Worded in another fashion, you need to get out of your own way. Free yourself for the leaping.

It is not enough to see the blockage for WHAT it is. You must learn WHY the blockage is there. You must further discover HOW to remove, or by-pass, the blockage.

The Kangaroo Factor – Dream Big! Think Big! Seize The Moment! will enable you to recognize the BIG WHAT, the blockage, as the thievery that it is. This book will help you research the blockage and discover yourself as the BIG WHY. It will then help you respond with a HUGE HOW as you develop your own leaping system.

This book will help you get out of your own way. It will help you have huge dreams, think productive thoughts, and translate your positive attitudes into productive behavior. You will not only see yourself as the chief source of blockage in general. You will specifically discover your choice to live in Could City rather than in Do City as a major blockage-factor. You will discover specific steps for blasting the blockage away. You will learn how to move to Do City.

An Introduction

I want you to enter this book fully understanding that you can choose to live in one of two distinct cities. We will be defining Could City as that harried habitat of Doubt and Postponement. We will be defining Do City as that environs painted with Defined Destiny, Decisive Direction, Dogged Determination, and Distinctive Delight.

I want you to enter this book fully aware of the fact that it, without apology, challenges you to value your choices. It challenges you to validate your potential. This bears repeating. The mission of *The Kangaroo Factor* is twofold. It challenges you to *value* your power to choose. It challenges you to *validate* your potential.

The responsibility for using, or not using, these ideas is entirely yours. These are only ideas. They are not law. They are not demands. The ideas in *The Kangaroo Factor* are a composite of my observations and reflections over the past three decades. How you respond to them is entirely your choice.

As you exercise your choice-power, you will *stop deceiving* and *start achieving*. As you discover afresh the satisfaction of taking responsibility for your own abilities and behavior, you will *stop robbing* yourself and *start rewarding* yourself. You will

THE KANGAROO FACTOR

"be" you. Your doing will extend out from your being. You, my friend, will leap. You will soar! You will be freed from your postponement-pouch.

The Kangaroo Factor – Dream Big! Think Big! Seize The Moment! is divided into five parts. The five basic parts of this book are:

- Choose Your City
- Delight In Your Dream
- Target Your Thoughts
- Seize Your Moments
- Celebrate The Cycle

Part One, Choose Your City, simply states that there are two cities from which you can choose. You can choose to live in one of them. Ultimately, you cannot live in both of them at the same time. The cities equal Could City and Do City. The two main streets that run through Could City are Doubt and Postponement. The four main streets that intersect Do City are Defined Destiny, Decisive Direction, Dogged Determination, and Distinctive Delight. You will choose to live in one of these cities. No one else will put you there. You select your spot. You choose your city. You will be encouraged to choose wisely.

An Introduction

Part Two, Delight In Your Dreams, will challenge you to gorge yourself during the Dream Banquet. It beckons you to take pleasure in huge dream-slices. Taste the delectable visions; enjoy the appetizing imaginations. Experience extravagance. There will be no "doggie-bag," no "to-go box," no "leftovers." You will be encouraged to savor it all!

Part Three, Target Your Thoughts, calls you to aim high, to point positively, to target your best outcomes. Quite simply, it challenges you to think about the thoughts you think. It treats negative thoughts, the thoughts that torture, with disdain. It encourages you to throw those very thoughts in the dump. It treats positive thoughts, thoughts that need to triumph within your very head and heart, with respect. It encourages you to take these thoughts and put them in the bank. It lambastes tiny thinking and lauds tremendous thinking. It cautions about the venom that travels with diluted and polluted thoughts. It exhorts dreamers to absorb huge doses of positive and productive thought.

Part Four, Seize Your Moments, is an invitation to grasp with every fiber within you the opportunity to leap. It requests hugeness on your part. It offers back to you heap upon heap of meaning and satisfaction. It reminds you that if you do not seize and

THE KANGAROO FACTOR

manage your moments, then your moments may equal mystery, perhaps even misery. Seize Your Moments challenges you to sculpt excellence, to craft your finest, to mold your best. It urges you to make the most of every spectacular moment of opportunity. It also encourages you to make the very most of every single life-moment with which you are gifted. It exhorts "mastery" for you as that awesome activity where your best becomes that which is perpetually redefined. You set the bar. You reach the bar. You raise the bar. The cycle continues.

Part Five, Celebrate The Cycle, is the hoisting of a huge flag with winds hurling its banner-words on every side of life's pole: IT HAS ONLY JUST BEGUN. I HAVE NOT SEEN MY BEST YET. I CAN LEAP HIGHER AND FURTHER STILL! There are bigger dreams and bigger thoughts yet. The moments that have been mastered may only foretell a hint of what is to come. This grand life can indeed be perpetually redefined. In reality, the cycle of celebration is rarely a single event. It normally equals process.

I have written this introduction in such a fashion as to allow it to serve a dual role for you. Certainly, it launches our time together. It also, perhaps more effectively than any of my previous

An Introduction

introductions, can serve as a quick review of the heart of the book. There is no doubt that you will want to wear-out the pages of this entire book. Work them. Question them. Write your notes on their faces. Highlight what will help you. Again, you are the driver here. Pay your read-and-study dues. Then visit A Treasury of Power Points in Chapter Fifteen, as well as this very introduction, for purposes of review.

The launching and review phases of this introduction will be enhanced as you are now presented with a further capsule of what is to come in the form of Eight Rules To Dream By.

A Capsule Of What Is To Come Eight Rules To Dream By

Define your dream. Avoid the land of "not knowing." Listen to your passion. Name and sculpt your dream by allowing your interests and talents to serve as a rudder for dream definition. Flex. Play to your strengths. When naming your dream, be very specific. Select "Start a landscape business" over "Go into business for myself." Choose "Write romance novels" over "Become an author." Decide

THE KANGAROO FACTOR

to "Become a world renowned pianist" rather than "Go into music." Choose to "Pursue computer animation" over "Study art."

See your dream happening! Harness the wonderful image your mind's eye is preparing for you. Visualize your dream bursting into life and confidently marching toward maturity. Give your dream every benefit of doubt you can muster on its behalf. View in your head and heart the way your world will look once you reach dream-accomplishment.

Excite and ignite. Give your named and visualized dream a wake-up call. Enhance your passion with an enthusiastic dream-commencement. Call in your "friend-force." Gift yourself and your dream with the inertia that an authentic and competent cadre of supporters has to offer. Excite your force of friends. Then receive a spark from them that will help your dream ignite and catch fire

Enjoy and expect. Enjoy the flow. Expect some detours. With dream in focus, with clarity of purpose at your side, you are ready for pursuit. You have every right to be excited about the journey and the dream. Stack the odds for success in your favor by orchestrating the journey so that it equals what you will enjoy, rather than what you will endure. Prepare for enjoyment, but also expect that at least

An Introduction

occasionally you will travel by detour. Anticipate some detours. Refuse to be caught off guard. Deny the detours any opportunity to rob you of your joy.

Seize your opportunities. Warning: Postponement-pouches will be everywhere. Watch out for them. Procrastination will wear camouflage. When appropriate opportunities for the advancement of your dream objective appear, leap for them. Do not analyze them to death. Swallow them whole. Maximize them. Gift yourself with systems that will allow you to make the most of every opportunity. Be very leery of opportunity-evaporation.

Monitor your thoughts. Think about the thoughts you think every step of your way. Remember that the thoughts you think impact the dreams you design. Discard your negative thoughts in the dump. Eliminate them. Do not allow them to trash your dream. Deposit your positive thoughts in the bank. Keep them around so they can continue to service your journey. Relate to your "thought-life factor" as either a dream discourager or as a dream encourager. Value your "thought-life factor" as either a dream breaker or a dream maker. It is that important.

Bring home the dream. Finish what you started. Bring the dream-journey to a point of arrival.

THE KANGAROO FACTOR

Reach the destination. Touch "finishedness." Share the accomplishment with supportive home folk and with your force of friends. The completion and the sharing will prepare you for the final rule.

Celebrate the cycle. Ultimately, the realization of a dream does not equal an ending. It more closely resembles another beginning. Accomplishment gives way to anticipation. Finishedness invites the future. There is the hoisting of a huge flag that states, with an unabashed affirmation, "The best is yet to be."

As is my custom, I have included a recommended reading list for you to ponder. You will find included in this vast reservoir of books material that should touch and teach your mind and perhaps even your spirit. Again, choose what is useful or helpful to you. This is only a choice-list. You do the choosing.

In a very real sense, you do not have to do this alone. There is the ONE who Karl Barth calls the "Holy Other." There is the Father of us all, and there is Jesus Christ, His Son – ever alive. I want to be very careful and delicate here. I do not want to offend. Nor do I want to be manipulative. Some might disagree with me and choose to read no more. Others will agree and will read further for the reason of agreement alone. What I must say is that my dreaming, my

An Introduction

thinking, my seizing, my seeing, my being, and my doing is most authentic when it comes closest to being blessed with purity of motive, and when it comes closest to being grounded in His Spirit. I trust you know, or will discover, The One who is the source of our highest dreams, our purest thoughts, and our most authentic actions. To Him be the glory!

With that said, now do your part. Discard your postponement-pouch. Leap at the opportunity to grow. Stop robbing yourself. Pay yourself back with huge dreams, tremendous thoughts, moments seized, and moments mastered. And do it now.

Now, I encourage you to exercise your choice!

Choice (*chois*), n.: see Part One

Part One

Choose Your City

CHAPTER 1

Where Do You Want To Live?

For our purposes, the answer to the above is no ordinary country. It is not America or Australia. It is no ordinary state. It is not South Carolina or South Dakota. It is no ordinary city. It is not Anaheim or Atlanta. It is a state of mind. It is a city encompassing both attitude and behavior.

Let me set the stage for my thinking here by introducing you to Weezie. She is the most remarkable person I have ever known. I have met many leaders: a president, a chief of staff, a prime minister, and chief executive officers. None have come close to Weezie.

THE KANGAROO FACTOR

For one hundred and three years, Weezie blessed the North Georgia hills with a gentle directness, a subtle wit, and a classic grace. The strength of a giant emanated from her diminutive frame. In countless ways, I am the beneficiary of all that equaled Weezie, my grandmother. Weezie chose for herself a special world. She chose a Do City-World. Living life to its fullest was not that which she "could do." It was that which she "did do." She modeled integrity for me.

I want you to see her now. Barely five feet tall, and that with a stretch. Clad with broken spectacles mended only by a band-aid that seemed to last forever. Comforted by a rainbow-colored shawl over her knees and ankles.

Weezie was incessantly huggable, amazingly alert, hilariously funny. And, certainly, she was a words-crafter supreme. Weezie knew how to romance the nominative with the objective, to allow adjectives to flirt with nouns, to distinguish verbs by degree or manner with adverbs! And did she ever know the significance and the power of one single word!

It is this "significance of a single word" that brings us back to Weezie just a few months after her passing. Our family was keenly aware of Weezie's

Where Do You Want To Live?

appreciation for Elizabeth Barrett Browning. Accordingly, the gentleman responsible for the engraving on Weezie's monument was to inscribe on the monument Weezie's favorite Elizabeth Barrett Browning quote – "How do I love thee? Let me count the ways!" Weezie was always affectionately quoting that to her children, her grandchildren, and her great-grandchildren.

Finally, the monument arrived. Apparently, the engraver was not as familiar with Elizabeth Barrett Browning as was Weezie. For you see, the monument did not read – "How *do* I love thee? Let me count the ways!" It read – "How *could* I love thee? Let me count the ways!" Oh, the difference one word can make! Let us now take that difference and apply it to our time together in this book.

Where Do You Now Live?

Are you at a point in your life where you are emphasizing the "do"? Or are you only emphasizing the "could"? Are you best described as being "determined" or "doubtful"? Are you going through life "doing" or merely "wondering if you ever could do"? Do you stand for the celebration of all that which has birthed "do" for you? Or do you sit and merely wait

THE KANGAROO FACTOR

for happy endings that "could" come? Do you leap high and far like the red kangaroo? Or, like a baby kangaroo, do you still live in mama's pouch, the postponement-pouch? Do you have a focus-bar, a rudder (like the kangaroo's tail)? Or do you live on the street called "Rudderlessness"?

Where are you now choosing to live? Which city do you now call home? Do City? Or Could City? Do you have success strategies? Or is that something that is still only part of your "could happen one day" world? Do you overcome adversity when it flies in your face? Or does adversity pummel you down to nothing but a "could happen one day" state? When asked about specific, measurable, and powerful goal setting, do you respond, "That is what I now do"? Or would you have to state, with hesitation, "Well, I guess that is what I could do, maybe"?

Will your monument statement be centered on "Do" or "Could"? Is dealing positively with change that which you do? Or is it that which you might could do? Is self-development that which you do? Or is it that which you might could do?

Do you live in Do City? Or do you live in Could City? These are very important questions. Could City could do you much more harm than good!

Where Do You Want To Live?

Who Decides Whether Or Not You Move?

You do! If you move from Could City to Do City it will be because you choose to do so. There is but one person who can ultimately take responsibility for your attitudes and your behaviors. You are that person! You choose to remain pinned in your postponement-pouch. Or you choose to leap out from your postponement-pouch.

> **There is but one person who can ultimately take responsibility for your attitudes and behaviors. YOU are that person!**

For sure, your parents gifted you with birth. Your Heavenly Father gifted you with abilities that will never be cloned, not even in one other person among billions. But if there is to be a meaningful life after birth, if there is to be an actualization extending out from your abilities, you must "will it" to happen. If you are to move from Could City to Do City, then

THE KANGAROO FACTOR

you must take responsibility for your choices! Like it or not, you were created to be a choice person.

For our purposes, there are at least two things that differentiate you from everyone else. One difference is "the given." "The given" equals your talents, your skills, your abilities. A second difference is "the gathered." "The gathered" equals the inspiration, the information, the insights you choose to gather from your relationships with others. It equals events, study, and the journey of exploration.

Now, these differences are interwoven. Only you can choose to use, or choose not to use, your abilities. Only you can choose to enhance, or choose not to enhance, your abilities. Only you can choose to learn, or choose not to learn, new skills.

How you choose to respond to your GIVEN and how you choose to GATHER determines your GROWTH. The GIVEN plus the GATHERED equals the GROWTH. This formula is central to your choosing. It is vital to your leaping. It must find center place within your head and heart. This formula must serve as a launching pad for big dreams, big thoughts, moments seized, and monuments mastered.

Where Do You Want To Live?

> **How you choose to respond to your GIVEN and how you choose to GATHER determines your GROWTH. The GIVEN plus the GATHERED equals the GROWTH.**

    We must remember that the glue that holds all of this together, or the fire that burns all of it apart, equals the very choices we make. I cannot overstate the power of our choices over our dreams, our thoughts, and our behavior.

> **The glue that holds all of this together, or the fire that burns it all apart, equals the very CHOICES we make.**

    Your very capacity to choose, to master existing abilities, or to seize new skills, clearly bestows upon you a robust responsibility. Handle it with respect. Your capacity to choose has everything to do with dreaming big, thinking big, seizing your moments, and mastering your moments. Do not take

THE KANGAROO FACTOR

your capacity to choose lightly! Exercise your right. Hold yourself accountable.

What Kind Of A Choice-Person Are You?

Do you choose to grow decisiveness within you? Or do you choose to breed little more than procrastination and postponement? Do you choose to leap? Or do you choose to remain in your postponement-pouch?

Your choices keep things from happening or they make things happen! As I have stated time and time again:

- Your choices create circumstances!
- Your choices confirm circumstances!
- Your choices change circumstances!

What you do with life has everything in the world to do with choices. What you do with your abilities has everything in the world to do with choices. Whether or not you sculpt your skills and maximize your performance has everything in the world to do with the choices you make.

Where Do You Want To Live?

Many of us do not see our dreams happening. We see our dreams not happening. This is very unfortunate. What we see, and what we do not see, has everything in the world to do with the choices we make.

> **Many of us do not see our dreams HAPPENING. We see our dreams NOT HAPPENING.**

Not By Accident

Stellar achievement rarely unfolds by accident. It happens because you choose it to happen. It is an "intentional occurrence." You can dream big if you intend to do so. You can think big if you intend to do so. You can seize the moment if you intend to do so.

Do not settle on a living site accidentally. Do not choose your city haphazardly. Do not leave it to chance. It should not be that tough of a choice. You must simply choose between Do City and Could City. You must simply choose between "Leaping-Land" and "Postponement-Pouch."

THE KANGAROO FACTOR

You ask yourself four simple and very important questions:

- What are the words on my life-monument?
- Do they read: "How do I …"?
- Do they read: "How could I …"?
- What are the "city street" names on which I will live?

Possible City Street Names

Do City	**Could City**
Ability Actualization	Ability Avoidance
Maximization	Mediocrity
Responsibility	Recklessness
Wisdom	Waste
Initiative	Inadequacy
Delight	Dread
Preparation	Postponement
Decisiveness	Doubt
Fulfillment	Frustration
Soaring	Survival
Mastery	Misery
Direction	Dilemma

One word, "Do" or "Could," can make a world of difference!

Where Do You Want To Live?

And So Can Time

Time can also make a world of difference.

More than three centuries ago, the first Europeans reached a special land. It was a turf that would later be named Australia. Upon arrival, these Europeans found themselves astonished by a peculiar-looking creature.

It was exceptionally gifted, not at walking or running, but at leaping. The Europeans were particularly drawn to its enormous feet, its large, and powerful hind limbs, its short fore limbs, and its massive and muscular tail.

The Europeans were so intrigued by this unusual being that they asked the native Australians (the Aborigines or the Koori), "What is the name of this animal?" The response they heard was, "Kangaroo." It meant, "I do not know." The name stuck.

Many decades after the Europeans first noticed the animal they would later call "kangaroo," scientists would find it necessary to bless the kangaroo family with a scientific name – "Macropodidae." The translation for "Macropodidae" is "big-footed." In other words, over a very long period of time, "I do not know," "I do not understand," was transformed or

THE KANGAROO FACTOR

expanded into "big-footed." Time had indeed made a world of difference.

The Kangaroo Factor underscores the transformation that can perpetually unfold within you and me. We can transcend our "do not knows" and our "do not understands." With a massive "big footedness" we can take big dream-steps. We can take big thought-steps. Our "big-footedness" can lead to moments seized and moments mastered. We do not have to stay the way we are. Time can indeed work to our advantage.

For our purposes, Could City equals little more than repeated "I do not know" statements. Could City equals habitual "I do not understand" responses. Could City equals a place where "not knowing" and "not understanding" confines people into postponement-pouches. Or, at best, it allows them to take only timid, tiny steps – always holding them close to their postponement-pouch.

However, Do City residents experience another world. It is a world where "not knowing" and "not understanding" hold little power. It is a world where timid, tiny steps give way to bold, big steps. Do City equals a marvelous, dream-crucible!

Where Do You Want To Live?

Back To Our Big Question

Where do you really want to live? Does one word, "Do" or "Could," now make a world of difference? Does time, your accumulated feelings and experiences in your own postponement-pouch, now make a world of difference for you? Are you now ready to move from confusion to clarity? Are you ready to exchange timid, tiny steps for bold, big steps?

Choose your city!

CHAPTER 2

Why Would You Choose Could City?

He asked, "Dad, what are you doing?"

"Leaving the drive-thru, Son. I have paid for the food."

"Yeah, Dad, but you do not have the food. How could you embarrass me like this?"

There was no answer. No rational answer. And now I ask you, "Is there any rational reason for choosing Could City?" Really now, why choose to leave the drive-thru before you receive your do-food, your big dreams, your big thoughts, your moments

THE KANGAROO FACTOR

seized, your moments mastered? Why leave it to saying, "I could always go back for it." Why live in the Could City of postponement? Do your big dreaming now! Do your big thinking now! Seize your moments now! Give into joy now!

Could City

Let me approach this from another perspective. The "could" I seek to describe tells the tale of leaving the drive-thru without the action-food. It carries tones of postponement! It equals an incessant having-to-go-back.

Worded another way, Could City does not equal action. It equals non-action. You may go through the motions (order and pay for the food), but you do not fully act (get the food)! It equals all of that good stuff left back at the drive-thru!

Why Leave The Good Stuff At The Drive-Thru?

Why leave the good stuff at the drive thru? Why live in an "I could always go back someday" world? Certainly, there is virtue in reflection. There

Why Would You Choose Could City?

is wisdom in time spent pondering. But places called Repeated Reflection and Perpetual Pondering are not places that you would want to call home all the time. If Repeated Reflection and Perpetual Pondering become your permanent residence, then "Could" rules over "Do" and you end up leaving the food of satisfaction and meaning back at the drive-thru!

Could City is a city polluted with postponement or procrastination. Your "Someday World" denies "Now" and "Seize" a place. Why would you want to live in a city like that? In Could City, you hear: "Whoa, Hold Off, Postpone, Doubt, Procrastinate, Stop." In Could City, you never hear: "Wow, Hurrah, Way To Go, Super."

Not only is Could City a polluted city. It is also a dark city. There are no excitement-lights, no accomplishment-lights, and no joy-lights! There is a great deal of slipping and tripping in Could City. Bruises are commonplace. Spirit-bones are often broken.

> **Could City is a DARK city. There are no excitement-lights, no accomplishment-lights, and no joy-lights!**

THE KANGAROO FACTOR

Why would you choose to live in Could City? You do not have to. You can leave the drive-thru with your Do-Food!

There Comes A Time

Kangaroos are marsupials (animals who nurture their young in a pouch). Initially, a baby kangaroo (a joey) lives entirely within the mother's pouch. Approximately five months into life, the joey will periodically peek out from the pouch. Sometimes he may eat some grass. About a month later, the joey will completely leave the pouch for brief moments. Often, he will jump back inside if a problem arises outside.

However, there comes a time when the joey will retreat to the pouch no more. In the case of the red kangaroo, that time frame is approximately eight months. For the gray kangaroo, the time frame is closer to ten months. It really does not matter whether it is eight months or ten months. There comes a time when the pouch is off limits!

In similar fashion, there comes a time when Could City is off-limits. There comes a time to leap toward another city. That other city, a much better city, is Do City! Do City does offer excitement-lights, accomplishment-lights, and joy-lights.

CHAPTER 3

Have You Thought About Do City?

Many years ago, one of our children was having difficulty with his homework. I decided to purchase a set of those study-tapes that I had seen advertised on television.

It did help, but not precisely as I had imagined. I imagined that the tape would arrive. I envisioned it being viewed rather quickly. That is not the way it happened. It seemed as if postponement was alive and well. The child ignored the tapes.

THE KANGAROO FACTOR

Then I became sick, very sick. I remember it vividly. Do you know the first thing this child did upon learning of my illness? He went in his room, shut the door, started studying the tapes. Just like that, he moved from Could City to Do City.

Only when that little boy saw his dad in the throes of kidney-stone pain did he move from "Could City" to "Do City." His motivation was pain, my pain. It was perhaps mixed with remorse and guilt – his remorse and his guilt.

I invite you to think of Do City before Could City causes you too much pain. Think seriously of Do City before guilt and remorse set in. If you have not thought of choosing Do City, then do it now! It will do you and your dream a world of good.

Pack Your Stuff

Pack your stuff. Put into your suitcase energy, excitement, enthusiasm. You are going to need them. Put in your bag direction, delight, determination, destiny. You are going to need them. Pack up your dreaming capacity, your thought-life engine, your choice-voice, your go-for-it-all suit.

Leave Could City and its postponement and self-inflicted doubt behind you. Travel the transition

Have You Thought About Do City?

road. Enjoy the ride. You will be going from indecision to decisiveness, from frustration to fulfillment. Head for Do City. Experience it as a dream-realization city. Appreciate it as a "system city."

Systems Over Symptoms

The next several chapters will lay out specific systems, or steps, for thriving in Do City. The systems *The Kangaroo Factor* exhorts will help you transcend the very symptoms of your frustration. You have every right to be excited about the supremacy of Do City systems over Could City symptoms.

Could City will never give you the chance to marry who you are to what you want to do in the exciting way Do City can! Could City will do nothing more than throw nasty symptoms your way. It hurls symptoms that do little more than stifle you. It breeds symptoms that indicate postponement or self-inflicted doubt. Really, that is all Could City has to offer you and your dream.

Read All About Do City

I encourage you to think about Do City. Think about its powerful systems. Do City offers you a

THE KANGAROO FACTOR

tremendous **See-It** System, an awesome **Be-It** System, and a powerful **Do-It** System. Think about Do City. Read its brochures. Read about big dreams, big thoughts, seizing the moments. Read about Do City. Read, then go. Go where you have never gone before. Love it! Leap your way to new trails. Soar toward productive landings.

> **Go where you have never gone before and LOVE it!**

One day, when someone asks you if you have ever been to Do City, I hope you can say "yes." I further hope that you can say, "I liked it so much, I decided to stay!" These next chapters will lay out for you attitude-systems and action-systems. These systems can cause you to feel grateful that you traveled to, and stayed in, Do City. Therefore, do not wait for the pain, the remorse, and the guilt.

Head for these Do City streets now: Defined Destiny, Decisive Direction, Dogged Determination, and Distinctive Delight. Get excited about these streets. Explore them. As you learn more about the Do City streets, through both the reading and the

Have You Thought About Do City?

exploring, you will find that your first Do City step is actually a define-your-dream leap.

> **You have every right to be EXCITED about being in Do City.**

You Are A City Manager

You manage a city. You oversee all of its departments. You supervise all that which equals mediocrity or excellence. In guiding your city, you preside and admonish. You maintain the status quo or you steer toward the new. You are the manager. You occupy the chair. You run the show. You call the shots and hold down the fort. You are city-boss!

What is the name of the city you manage? Is it one of a million names? No. It is one of two names. It is simple. You manage Could City. Or you manage Do City. There is no vacuum, no void, no neuter land. You manage one of these two cities.

Are you Could City manager? Are you in charge of postponement? Do you handle the doubt? Do you administer "what-if?" codes based on fear of the past?

THE KANGAROO FACTOR

Or do you pilot a city named Do City? Are big dreams, huge thoughts, and moments mastered apparent throughout your City Hall? Are your city-buildings named Purpose, Place, Power, and Passion? Are you steering a city named Do, a Hall of Fame city blessed with sub-divisions called Maximum Performance, Balanced Life, Phenomenal Service, and Dream Realized? Is the Do City you oversee blessed with excellence that is being perpetually redefined by you?

If you currently manage Do City, then congratulations. If you do not currently lead your own Do City of dreams, but would now like to take a critical first step, then congratulations to you as well.

The Kangaroo Factor is written for those of us who have postponed our dream fulfillment for far too long. It is a call to positive attitudes and positive dream-actions. It mandates a departure from the postponement-pouch. It requires a first step, a leaping maneuver, and a dream definition.

Part Two

Delight In Your Dream

CHAPTER 4

Give Your Dream A Name

I see him periodically at our local post office. We exchange pleasantries. Normally that is all. Then we move our separate ways. On this day it was different. He noticed me, approached me, and stopped. There was an incessant glare toward my chest. Finally, he stated, "I see you have also been a patient at the hospital." Since I have not stayed overnight in a hospital for more than forty-five years, I was taken back by his statement. I responded, "Excuse me?"

"Your jersey," he said.

I held back a smile and said, "Oh, Emory."

THE KANGAROO FACTOR

"Yes, Emory. That's my hospital, too," he responded.

"And, a fine hospital at that," I replied. I continued, "However, I wear my Emory jersey because I attended, and graduated from, Emory University."

Perhaps I should have said nothing. I must I admit I was somewhat taken back by his point of view. My acquaintance's perception of the Emory logo on a gray jersey was narrow. As far as he was concerned, the Emory logo referred to the hospital – Emory University Hospital. However, in a broad sense, the Emory logo referred to the University as a whole. "Emory" is liberal arts. It is philosophy and music. It is business and science. It is medicine, yes, but it is also theology and law. It is doctors and nurses, yes, but it is also coaches, bookstore clerks, student-government leaders, dormitory counselors, chaplains, and landscape architects. To think "Emory" is to think Emory University Hospital, yes. But, to think "Emory" is to think much more.

Understandably, but unfortunately, my post office buddy had a one-sided, short-circuited, tunnel-vision view of Emory. To him, when Emory was "embroidered" on the jersey, it meant "hospital." It did not mean anything else.

Give Your Dream A Name

In similar fashion, "dream" means one thing, and one thing only, to many people. To these persons, "dream" means "what you subconsciously do while you are asleep, normally at night." Dreams for them are ignited only during sleep. These people never walk the wide campus of productive "visioneering." The other side of dreaming is something they never get to know. They do not visit life's real dream-laboratories. They know little about those dreams that occur dramatically and powerfully while one is awake.

A larger view of dreaming shouts with unabashed affirmation: "Dreaming possesses an awake-life as well." To free yourself from boredom, mediocrity, or even the success-lock of your "as-is-ness," you must awaken yourself and your dream. In order to maximize your performance, you must wake up. You must dream precisely while you are awake. You must dream while you are alert. Dreaming must equal a conscious energy, a determined effort, a disciplined activity that you "will" to happen.

The dreaming we address here is an igniting. It is a combustion of positive attitude and productive behavior. It is no wild fancy, no vain indulging. Its activity is not delirious or destructive in nature. It is not harmful. Neither is it hallucinatory. We are not

THE KANGAROO FACTOR

interested here in a state of "pipe-dreaming." Nor are we journeying toward lands named "Cloud Nine," "The Rainbow's End," or "The Pot Of Gold."

The dreaming we exhort equals a productive "visioneering." It equals a "questioneering" grounded in the exciting, the meaningful, the possible, and the awesome. The high dream that calls, caresses, and challenges you has much to give you: place, power, purpose, poise, and passion. Your capacity to receive what your dream wants to give you will prove to be a central thrust in *The Kangaroo Factor*.

> **The high dream that calls, caresses, and challenges you has much to GIVE to you: place, power, purpose, poise, and passion.**

Your dream also demands much of you. It wants your intelligence, your ingenuity, your inertia, your integrity. You should not fret. You already have what it takes! You have the tools. You have the talent. You can take action. You can learn from other accessible sources.

Give Your Dream A Name

> **Your dream also DEMANDS much of you: your intelligence, your ingenuity, your inertia, your integrity. You should not fret, because you already have what it takes!**

Do not insult this powerhouse concept by merely nibbling at awake and alert dreaming. Dream big. See your dream happening. Do not doubt yourself out of achievement. It is my experience that many of us do precisely that. We doubt ourselves out of achievement. Let me word it like this: "We do not see our dream happening. We see our dream not happening." And what we see in our minds is often what we see in reality.

Our problem comes from one of two views:

1. We do not believe in awake and alert dreaming.
2. We doubt our own dream-ability.

Both problems can be solved when we confidently begin dreaming big, thinking big, and seizing big while we are awake and alert.

THE KANGAROO FACTOR

Start Your Dream Engine

Therefore, dream big. See it happening. Ignite your dream. Kindle it while you are awake and alert. Ladies and gentlemen of Do City, start your dream engines. Define your dream.

Yes, you must define your dream. You must give it a name. Ultimately, others cannot define your dream for you. Ultimately, events will not define your dream for you. You are responsible for defining your dream.

Before you can really dream, awake and alert, you must define your dream. Before you can see your dream happening, you must know what your dream is. The "knowing the dream" precedes the doing. The "defining the dream" precedes the determination. When you identify your dream, you position yourself for mastery.

Define Your Dream

Your first move is actually a giant question – "What is my dream?" Your "what?" has to come before your "how?" Your "what?" even has to come before your "why?"

Give Your Dream A Name

The definition of your dream is the rudder for your attitude and behavior. Your dream-definition, your dream name, is a barometer. It is that standard by which you measure or monitor growth.

When you ask yourself what your dream is, do not say what the Aborigines said to the first Europeans when they were asked the name of that peculiar animal. Remember, they said "kangaroo," meaning, "I do not know." Know your dream. Understand your dream. Give it a name.

So again I ask you, "What is your dream?" Naturally, no one but you can answer this question. I will, however, share with you ten other questions that will help you answer your big dream question:

- "Is my dream grounded in faith?"
- "Is my dream influenced by the desire to become 'my very best'?"
- "Is my dream informed by a desire to serve others?"
- "Is my dream that which can be celebrated in increments?"
- "Will the realization of my dream bring me joy without harming others?"
- "Does my dream allow me to focus on my creative passion?"

THE KANGAROO FACTOR

- "Will the realization of my dream fill me with a 'wow' and a 'whew'?"
- "Can this dream yield itself to focus, fulfillment, and fun?"
- "Is my dream both an extension of my God-given talents and a recognition of my limits?"
- "Will this dream help me go to bed most nights with satisfaction and wake up most mornings with excitement?"

These questions, and your answers, will assist you in asking your big-dream questions. They can also help you answer your big-dream questions.

> **Ask yourself, "Will this dream HELP me go to bed most nights with satisfaction, and wake up most mornings with excitement?"**

Your Dream-Life

Call your dream something. Give your dream a name. Remember, your dream-life is not only nocturnal in nature. It is not merely a subconscious

Give Your Dream A Name

endeavor. Your dream-life can benefit you while you are awake and alert. Just as the "Emory" on my jersey represented not only the hospital but also the university, so can "dream" mean much more than sleep activity. It can equal a vigor for life, for achievement, for leaping, and for soaring.

Your capacity to dream, both awake and alert, demands a first step! Your first step is: GIVE YOUR DREAM A NAME. Write it down. Then go to it.

Your dream-name may mean much more than you ever imagined.

CHAPTER 5

Give Your Dream A Wake-Up Call

It happened in a sandbox in my backyard near a big old tree. I was five years old – alone. I can almost feel the sand between my toes now; I remember it that well. Something came over me that day. I will attempt to describe it.

My sandbox was blessed with newly painted wood sides, fresh sand, a plastic yellow shovel, and a red pail. Plastic firemen, army soldiers, and cowboys were strewn all over the sand. So, I guess it was only natural that I would be reflecting on my future.

THE KANGAROO FACTOR

"I would be a fireman. . . a soldier. . . no, a cowboy." Fantasies floated from one to the other. And then it happened.

It was not a voice, or anything like that. It was a feeling – "I would be a businessman." That feeling carried with it a peace and a confidence that was almost unimaginable.

However, peace and confidence in relationship to my career-dream began to elude me during my high school years. They were replaced with uncertainty – and a massive dose of inferiority.

At the time, I rationalized that my dream-confidence was eroding because of what they (my classmates) and others were doing to me:

- They were calling me "skinny."
- They would not let me in the Key Club.
- They would choose me last while we played backyard football.
- They would tease me more than I deserved to be teased.

I even remember being told what my father said to my mother as I was walking across the stage on high school graduation night: "Why is he strutting so? He hasn't done anything special!"

Give Your Dream A Wake-Up Call

I wondered, "How could he talk like that?" Now I think he was right. Little was coming together for me. No huge nightmare, but no "sandbox confidence and serenity" either.

The uncertainty that was floating within began to equal a huge uncertainty that extended toward my career. That uncertainty revealed itself in school after school and in career after career.

In reality, the businessman-dream I had greeted earlier with peace and confidence would only resurface decades later. All of my history would culminate in, and actually benefit, a fulfilling career in business. However, I had to experience some "woe" before I could experience some "go" for the dream.

My "go" only overpowered my "woe" when I took responsibility for my choosing-power and stopped blaming my struggle on "them" and "it." I made the choice to discard my shift-the-blame button.

"Go" will overpower "woe" when you take RESPONSIBILITY for your choosing power and stop blaming your struggle on "them" and "it."

THE KANGAROO FACTOR

"Woe" As Tutor

If "woe" equals a frustrating "where you have been" for you, if "woe" equals an incessant "traveling by detour" for you, or even if "woe" equals too much time in the postponement-pouch for you, then please remember these two points:

- Your past can be a great teacher.
- You do not have to stay the way you are.

Not only can your past befriend you with a world of valuable lessons, it can also invite you and encourage you to go for your dream. For sure, "woe" will not hide forever. (That has certainly not been my experience – even to this day.) But when you give in to joy, when you dream big, think big, and seize your moments, "woe" will take backseat to "go." Heaps of frustration will take backseat to the fulfillment-leap.

> **When you give in to joy, when you dream big, think big, and seize your moments, "woe" will take back-seat to "GO."**

Give Your Dream A Wake-Up Call

I like to think about that old sandbox from time to time. For me, that sandbox is where the dream started. And I believe that the dream over the years has touched my life in areas that transcend work. Whether it is from a sandbox or a sanctuary, whether it is from a stadium or a suburban home, whether it is in a classroom or at corporate headquarters, you can experience your dream's starting point time and again. You can view, and review, your dream's starting point as a tool for "rediscovery" and "reenergizing."

With dream "seed-point" in head and heart, you find yourself prepared to do two things.

- You give your dream a name.
- And then you give your dream a wake up call.

Anon, Anon

If my understanding is correct, St. Augustine and I have something in common. Oh, for sure, I do not refer to intellect or insight. There I do not even come close.

If there is any point of commonality between us, it has to do with our attitudes about getting up in

THE KANGAROO FACTOR

the morning. Quite simply, he did not want his mother to wake him up in the morning. When she would attempt to do so, he would, sometimes with massive doses of vigor, respond, *"Anon, anon."* Translated, "anon, anon" basically means "not now, not now."

The question you and I must face is this: "In relationship to our dream's wake-up call, have we been responding for far too long with '*anon, anon*' – 'not now, not now?'"

Have you "not now-ed" yourself to the point of despair? Have you "not now-ed" yourself to the point of misery? Then stop it. It may be time to leave the postponement-pouch.

A Word Of Caution

This particular sub-heading will be very brief, but it is extremely important. We must understand that there will be times when "not now" is appropriate. Just as the baby kangaroo should remain within his mother's pouch for several months before he even peeks his head out, so must we, from time to time, decide that "not now" is indeed the appropriate response. Just as it is not wise for the kangaroo to leave his mother's pouch too early, so can it be inappropriate for us to proceed with a project "too early."

Give Your Dream A Wake-Up Call

Selectively Use Your Snooze

With the above caution stated, let us now address that highly tempting device. It is called the "snooze" button.

You have a named dream. You own your dream. This very book may be the alarm clock. Unless it is appropriate, do not even think about pressing the "snooze" button. Unless it is appropriate, do not even think about saying "anon, anon" – "not now, not now." Unless it is appropriate, do not even think about retreating to the postponement-pouch.

Awaken your dream. Go back to the dream-naming spot. (For me it was the sandbox.) Now you are ready for further exploration into Do City.

CHAPTER 6

Give In To Joy

To grow up as a young 'un in the South in the fifties was quite an experience. For example, a typical scenario might unfold like this.

A young man would take a fancy to a young lady. The fancy might even equal a mild flirting. All would be fine – fine that is until another young man would appear. And he would be interested in the same young lady. The first young man would become jealous; then he would become defensive. He would flex and flaunt his muscles. Tension would

THE KANGAROO FACTOR

be created between the two young men. A fight would develop.

Eventually, one young man would emerge as the winner of the fight. There would be no objective judging of the fight. There would be no scoring. The fight's end would occur because one young man would finally say, "I give." Of course what he really was saying was, "I give in to pain. I do not like the position I am in. I am tired of the humiliation and the hurt." The "professionals" might refer to this as a "submission hold." You and I might more readily refer to it as an "I can take no more of this hold." In this instance, the "I give" is brought on by an overdose of pain blended with a "no way out" feeling. The one-two punch that leads to the throwing in of the towel equals pain piled upon perceived hopelessness.

The number of persons who submit to the onslaught of hurt is legion. The number of one-time dreamers who surrender to the perceived humiliation of failure or fear is mind-boggling. These persons eventually feel as if "dreaming while you are awake and alert" is not for them.

Give In To Joy

WD

For more than a decade, it was my privilege and pleasure to teach public speaking on the college level. Almost every quarter, when the official and final roll was presented to me, one or more names would be followed by those very frustrating letters "WD" – withdrew. For sure, schedules and other circumstances would often mandate a change. But on many occasions I would wonder, "Did the student withdraw because he felt that he was trapped or caught? Did the student give in to pain and perceived hopelessness?" I hate it when dread or despair wins. Unfortunately, during those years, I think it did win from time to time.

The Kangaroo Factor shouts with unabashed affirmation: "Submission and withdrawal are not the only options."

There Is Another Option

For most of my adult life, I have been sharing one particular quote from Henry David Thoreau: "The mass of men live in quiet desperation." I am afraid that is the only Thoreau quote many people know. There is another relevant Thoreau quote that

THE KANGAROO FACTOR

must be considered, just as there is another response than "giving in to pain and despair" that must be pondered. The last three sentences that form the conclusion of Thoreau's *Walden* read: "Only that day dawns to which we are awake. There is more day to dawn. The sun is but a morning star."

Naturally, the dream-response that should be evoked within each of us is not that of dread, but that of joy. The "submission-hold" need not reign superior. You and I do not have to give in to despair. Discouragement does not have to become the victor. There is something else. Submitting to broken dreams, to half-heartedness, to an incessant "less than my best" is not your only option. Being held captive in the postponement-pouch by an army of "I do not knows" is not the only option. With confidence and clarity, you can leap forward with big dream steps and big thought steps. Thoreau was right. There is "more day to dawn." Dreamer, keep telling yourself that!

**The "submission-hold" need not reign superior.
You and I do not have to give in to despair.
There is ANOTHER OPTION.
It equals a confident "leaping and landing."**

Give In To Joy

You Can Give In To Joy

Here, "give in" has nothing in the world to do with submitting – if submitting only means quitting. Here "give in" means receive, experience, enjoy. Not only can you give your dream a name, not only can you give your dream a wake up call, you can give in to joy. You can give joy to your dream. You can enjoy both the dream and the dreaming. You can delight in your dream. Dreaming is much more productive when you enjoy it.

When I say "delight in your dream," what does that mean to you? When I say, "Delight in your dream," am I saying, "Delight in the accomplishment of your dream"? Not exclusively so. When I say, "Delight in your dream," am I saying, "Delight in the sigh of relief you breathe"? Not exclusively so. When I say, "Delight in your dream," am I saying, "At all costs it must always be destination-determination over journey-satisfaction"? Definitely not.

Let me attempt to explain myself in another fashion here. Do you believe that dream-joy is related exclusively to one moment – completion-moment, finish-moment, achievement-moment? Do you even believe that dream-joy is related exclusively to all that is made possible by the accomplishment of the

THE KANGAROO FACTOR

dream? Is dream-joy only the composite of finished-ness and results?

Before I experience dream-joy, must I first encounter absolute drudgery, total dread, submission-hold after submission-hold? Does dream-joy equal only game's end-moments and a celebration party?

Now, please understand me here. There is nothing wrong with destination-determination, goal-orientation, and event-focusing. However, there is something wrong when one gives in to a joy that equals only dream-destination and only post-destination moments.

The dream-joy behind *The Kangaroo Factor* is larger than goal-reached and goal-rewarded. For sure, dream-joy encompasses a goal reached and a goal rewarded. But it is not limited to that which is reached and to that which is rewarded. Dream-joy is larger than this. When I encourage you to give in to dream-joy, I hope you see the wide view. I do not want you to hold to a constricted version of dream-joy.

Dream-joy includes the journey, a journey whose rudder points toward achievement and post-achievement moments. However, it is not dependent upon those moments for ultimate meaning. I once heard a man who is now a bishop in the United

Give In To Joy

Methodist Church (Dr. Bevel Jones) say something like this, "We are called to be faithful, not necessarily successful." I interpret that to mean that our faithfulness to the dream-journey is crucial. Joy can be rooted in the journey.

Joy need not be confined to journey's end. To the contrary, journey's end is most quickly and easily reached when the very pursuit of the dream equals joy. Journey-joy does not erode destination-joy. Journey-joy enhances destination-joy.

> **Joy need not be confined to journey's end. To the contrary, journey's end is most quickly and easily reached when the very PURSUIT of the dream EQUALS JOY.**

Celebrate Incremental Finishedness

To give in to joy is to smile at the little steps of progress. It is to understand that there is joy in celebrating incremental finishedness. I encourage you to give in to the joy that is journey-centered. Do not only celebrate the touchdown. Celebrate the first

THE KANGAROO FACTOR

down. Celebrate the fourth and one. Do not only celebrate director-status. Celebrate the steps along the way. Enjoy not only your retirement. Enjoy your work! Stop putting all of your joy-eggs into a "one moment" achievement-basket. Success equals not only the destination. It equals journey-steps as well. It equals not only the landing. It also equals the leaping.

> **Stop putting all of your dream-eggs into a "one moment" achievement-basket. Success equals not only the destination. It equals JOURNEY-STEPS as well.**

Enjoy The Leaping And The Landing

Observe a leaping kangaroo. Notice the front legs brought in toward the body. View the calmness of movement. See how relaxed the kangaroo appears. Notice the tail high in the air, functioning like a rudder. Find yourself amazed at how graceful the kangaroo appears, as if it actually enjoys the leaping as much as the landing!

Give In To Joy

You too can experience and enjoy both the leaping and the landing associated with your dreams. The ratio between dream-journey satisfaction and dream-destination satisfaction equals the core of potential unleashed. One barrier many of us self-impose is this: "It is appropriate to enjoy dream-realization. It is inappropriate to enjoy dream-journey." Nonsense.

Learn to enjoy them both. The ratio between the two must equal a balancing. Take either strength too far and what you have ultimately equals a barrier.

If you become too preoccupied with dream-destination, you may find the preponderance of your life and your family starving for attention. There is nothing wrong with being dream-centered. Certainly, you must keep your eyes focused on your dream-target. But if you never allow your family and the whole of your person to be valued, if your never take your eyes off of your dream-destination-target, if you never rest your eyes, then your eyes suffer with a fatigue factor. When that happens, your dream-target actually blurs.

If you become too preoccupied with journey-servicing, if you sit around and wait for happy endings, if you fail to gift yourself with dream-destination and dream-determination (dream-discipline), then

THE KANGAROO FACTOR

you are rudderless. Journey is strangling your spirit, not servicing it.

You must occasionally gift yourself with dream-achievement. When you gift yourself with dream-achievement, you infuse into yourself an air of expectation centered around your very next journey!

A Balancing Act

To give in to joy is to balance your dream-journey with dream-satisfaction. You must value both. Difficulty may certainly be present. It need not, however, deny you joy. Appropriate balancing will take some of "the sting" out of the difficulty.

> **To give in to joy is to BALANCE your dream-journey with dream-satisfaction.**

To give in to joy is also to balance vocation with avocation, work-focus with life-focus. It is my firm experience that balancing of this breed does not detract from dream-realization. It enhances dream-realization.

Give In To Joy

The giving in to dream-joy that I describe is two foci. Again and again, journey and destination, vocation and avocation, work-focus and family-focus, must be balanced. The adhesive that will most effectively hold the two together is faith.

At this writing, I feel that I have adequately addressed journey-joy. Let me now exhort the remarkable payoffs that occur when dream-destination-joy is reached and experienced.

Dream-Destination-Joy

Dream-destination-joy in the highest form includes the following:

- Satisfaction – "I have done this."
- Self-Confidence – "I can do other things like this."
- Service – "I am being used in a meaningful way."
- Significance – "There is value in this and value in me."
- Surprise – "There is more to me than I imagined."
- Suggestion – "Perhaps something larger is around the corner."
- Someone Else – "I have been gifted by a Higher Power."

THE KANGAROO FACTOR

Stop fighting Satisfaction and Self-Confidence. Quit battling Service, Significance, and Surprise. Cease your wrestling with Suggestion and Someone Else. Give in to joy. Enjoy the leaping and the landing!

Satisfaction

Satisfaction is a dangerous venom if it indicates contentment or even success-lock. Success-lock equals that preoccupation with the present that jeopardizes newness and growth. Satisfaction can put at risk a soaring that transcends success.

However, each of us, from time to time, needs to experience a huge "Yes," a resounding "Well Done," the validation of "Mission Accomplished." The satisfaction that travels along with dream-realization shouts: "Yes, Well Done, Mission Accomplished."

Each of us needs to EXPERIENCE a huge "Yes," a resounding "Well Done," the validation of "Mission Accomplished."

Give In To Joy

Self-Confidence

Satisfaction breeds self-confidence. When you give in to dream-joy, you gift yourself. You gift yourself not only with satisfaction, but also with a confidence emanating out from yourself. You celebrate, without embarrassment and without hesitation: "I did this once; I can do it again."

You have not found confidence. Confidence found you first. It found you by the way of prior satisfaction. It refuses to whisper to you, but shouts to you: "The best is yet to be. There is much more ahead. The pouch-departure is only the beginning."

Ultimately, you do not find confidence. Confidence FINDS YOU as you pay the preparation price.

Service

The joy that you give in to is MOST CHERISHED when it directly benefits others. When you are placed in a position to help others, you become a beneficiary as well. When "others-centered" dreams

THE KANGAROO FACTOR

reach fruition, there is a mutual benefit. There is a benefit for the one who receives, and there is a benefit for the one who gives. Experience the "service-related" feeling here. You will want to clone it. You will want to expand it.

Significance

The joy that sojourns with a realized dream attests not merely to your doing; it attests to your being. What you have done, the dream you have realized, is significantly celebrated by you as an extension of your being. (Please remember that dreams do not always have to be "completed" in order to be "celebrated" and "significant.")

Surprise

Due to the fact that we have repeatedly given in to doubt, drudgery, despair, and defeat, we have become conditioned for small, joyless dreams. Therefore, when dreaming big pays dividends, both along the way and at way's end, we are surprised. We say to ourselves: "This is different. I am giving in to joy. I am now experiencing something special: dreaming big, thinking big, seizing the moment. I am

Give In To Joy

no longer bound to my 'postponement-pouch.' I am now surprised at the freedom with which I can leap and soar."

Suggestion

The self-confidence related to dream-completion travels by the way of a simple suggestion. This simplicity refuses to diminish, but actually enhances, directness and vividness. It shouts: "Something larger may be just around the corner."

Someone Else

Often, one of our grandest surprises may be that we did not totally accomplish the dream by ourselves. We may feel as if we were "carried through" to dream-fulfillment. A plethora of others, and most especially our Heavenly Father, have gifted us with energy, effort, and fruit. In the highest sense, we have been the beneficiaries of Someone Else.

Enjoy The Process

Give in to joy – joy of process, joy of event. Give in to joy – joy of journey, joy of arrival. Dream

THE KANGAROO FACTOR

big. Enjoy your dream. Enjoy both the pursuit and the realization. Never allow your dream to be completely isolated to an event. Remember that dream-joy also encompasses a process.

Do your own balancing act. Run the course. Whenever possible, smile at the sweat. Give in to joy during your race.

At race's end, value: Satisfaction, Self-Confidence, Service, Significance, Surprise, Suggestion, and Someone Else. Have a blast. Give in to joy!

Our Recurring Theme

Before I conclude this last chapter in Part Two of *The Kangaroo Factor*!, I want to address a theme that will consistently reveal itself in our time together.

The adhesive that will connect the remainder of this book to the preceding pages is the following: "**Any effective dream-manager must be able to pass the "8-D Test."** The "8-D Test" equals:

- Discern
- Design
- Differentiate
- Drop

Give In To Joy

- Delegate
- Do
- Discipline
- Delight

The concept that will continue to ooze through the chapters of this book equals the fact that individuals who dream big, think big, and seize their moments have identified and implemented the eight components of the "8-D Test."

Although I have structured the book in such a fashion as to allow for restatement and enhancement of these eight elements, it is most helpful for them to be presented here.

Discern

It is impossible to give a name to one's dream, to give a wake up call to one's dream, or to give in to dream-joy unless one fully understands "discernment."

For our purposes, dream-discernment equals the act of recognizing, with reasonable clarity, the difference between a dream that will hurt one's self and one that will help one's self. Dream-discernment equals the activity of seeing, with some vividness, the

THE KANGAROO FACTOR

difference between a dream that is fundamentally wrong (in that it hurts others) and a dream that is right (because it helps others).

The dream-discernment test always comes in the form of understanding: "Do I understand this dream as that which allows for the very extension of my personality? Do I understand this dream as a possibility which, if realized, allows me to make the most of my skills, enhance my skills, even gift myself with new skills?"

To discern in relationship to one's dream is to ask with all of one's heart, with all of one's valued second opinions, and with all of Divine Guidance: "Is this dream of legitimate and high pursuit? Will this dream allow me to help others – not hurt others? Will it allow me to 'sing my song'? Or will I be 'barking up the wrong tree'?"

Design

Once your dream has been thoroughly filtered by your capacity to discern, once it passes the discernment-test, you are free for dream-design. Your dream-discernment exercise has gifted you with the Power Of Three: Excitement, Energy, Enthusiasm. You are ready to sculpt, or design, your dream:

Give In To Joy

- You give your dream its name.
- You visualize your realized dream and draw it.
- You share your dream with others who are important to you.
- You give your dream a wake up call.
- You take your huge dream and chunk it down into little dreams. You enjoy the chunking-down.
- You sequence your little dreams. You prioritize them up until the point of finishedness.
- You take the brakes off. You press the accelerator. You dream big.
- You plan; you prepare. You pursue; you progress. You pause; you pursue afresh.
- You give in to joy.
- You enjoy the leaping and the landing.

Differentiate

At this point, your pursuit surfaces as a wonderful teacher. You have discerned your dream. You have designed your dream. The pursuit-phase of your design-test drive begins to reveal something very important to you. Your pursuit teaches you this: "I had best learn to differentiate."

THE KANGAROO FACTOR

You sense this is the lesson your pursuit has for you because something has gone awry. The smooth flow you expected is absent. Your dream-journey is loaded with too many detours. You suspect that it is time to differentiate.

Detours in the design of your plan will always occur. Indeed, sometimes they should occur. Detours are not always dream-enemies. Detours may actually prove to be dream-friends because they may call you to differentiate. Detours may serve as wake-up signals.

> **Detours are not always dream-enemies. Detours may actually prove to be dream-friends because they may call you to DIFFERENTIATE.**

Detours can be for good. Detours can be for bad. Detours can help. Detours can hurt. Dream-detours can actually take you to a higher and better dream-place.

However, detours often result in significant dream-damage. Therefore, if one can diminish the number of damaging detours (or mistakes, or poor choices, or mismatches), then that one is more likely

Give In To Joy

to reach dream's goal. That one is also more likely to enjoy the dream-journey.

If you want to get the most out of your dream-design, your dream-pursuit, and your dream-realization, then you will want to minimize distractive and destructive detours. Differentiation is a wonderful way to deal with your detours. Differentiation makes it possible for you to learn, leap, and land!

You differentiate the helpful from the hurtful, the vital from the optional, when you ask the simple but powerful "differentiating" question: "Is this smaller part of the big dream something that I should Drop, Delegate, or Do?" You seek to arrange or "sort" the various segments of your dream into little dream steps. The segmenting, the differentiating, facilitates your categorizing.

Please do not underestimate how important it is for you to bring the tremendous tool known as DIFFERENTIATION to the DETOURS that you face along your way.

In a world where detours may equal a total waste of time, the effective dream manager knows what little dream-step detours to DROP. In an environment where some detours equal necessary but exceptionally awkward steps, the effective dream manager knows when to DELEGATE activity to

THE KANGAROO FACTOR

another. Finally, when detours equal essential steps that no one else can walk, the effective dream manager will sometimes differentiate and conclude: "This I must DO!"

Drop

Some little dream-steps simply will not work. They are not productive. They are counter-productive. Normally, you will recognize when a particular step is not working, when it is inappropriate. If you are in doubt, you can, of course, seek second opinions, third opinions, and professional help. It is not smart to pursue a step that is shouting to your internal mandates: "Stop! I will not work! Drop me!"

Delegate

On occasion, a little dream-step is too important to be dropped. However, it is a crucial, little step that does not match your feet. This step could be a step requiring feet larger than your feet, or it could be a step requiring feet smaller than your feet. However, you determine that whatever the step-size, it is not your step-size.

Give In To Joy

An effective dream-manager will delegate a dream-step to one for whom the step-size is more appropriate. Once again, differentiation, and even discernment, come into play here. You must know WHEN TO ASK FOR HELP. You must know WHOM TO ASK FOR HELP. And, when appropriate, you must delegate, or out-source.

> **An effective dream-manager will DELEGATE a dream-step to one for whom the step-size is more appropriate.**

Do

The third level of the differentiation-test equals a word that embodies the very heart of our time together: DO. Do give into joy! Do dream big! Do think big! Do seize the moment! Do stop procrastinating! Do leap out of your postponement-pouch!

Do choose to live in Do City. Do choose to manage Do City. Do give your dream a name. Do give your dream a wake up call. Do learn the "8-D System." Do pass the "8-D Test." Do this step!

THE KANGAROO FACTOR

"Do" presents you with your third differentiation option, your third separation-choice, your third way of breaking down your little dream-steps.

An effective dream manager knows when to **drop** and stop ineffective dream-steps. A wise dream manager knows when to **delegate** little dream-steps to another person – one with a much better step-match. And finally, the dream manager who sizzles and soars knows when to say: "Yes, this is me. This is my step to take. This I will **do**!"

Discipline

If you drop certain dream segments, do not incessantly pick them back up again. Do not make it a habit to retrieve what you have dropped. Restraint on your part demands discipline.

If you choose to delegate and then repeatedly "look over your shoulder," then that activity will prove disheartening to all involved. Delegation need not require total relinquishment. However, it does require some distance on your part. Often, that distance will mandate your discipline.

If your DO is to be successful, then your do-effort must be informed and influenced by discipline. Your do-efforts must be nourished with a regimen

Give In To Joy

that equals passion, preparation, determination, and resiliency. There is little room for timidity, faint-heartedness, or a wishy-washy behavior.

The one who drops, delegates, and does always has a middle initial. The one who dreams big, thinks big, and seizes the moment always has a middle initial. The middle initial is "D." The "D" stands for discipline. Discipline yourself.

Delight

And delight yourself!

Discipline can certainly result in delight at dream's end. However, the one who dreams big, thinks big, seizes the moment, the one who understands the discipline of mastery, will pass the Delight-test in two instances. This occurs not only when dream-destination is reached, but during dream-journey as well.

The delight offered by *The Kangaroo Factor* is two-foci: dream-journey and dream-destination. This delight is also cyclical in nature. The Do City Manager, the effective dream manager, experiences a wonderful enigma: the enigma of dream-reached. Dream-reached need not equal closure or cessation. Dream-reached calls for new dream-journey!

THE KANGAROO FACTOR

Worded another way, delight in journey leads to delight at destination point. Delight at destination-point invites another dream-journey. And the cycle can continue. This is true with little dream-steps as well as big dream-steps. Series can be piled upon series. Cycles can be stacked upon cycles. And the process can continue!

The Process

A huge dream is designed. The "8-D Test" (discern, design, differentiate, drop, delete, do, discipline, and delight) unfolds. A city is chosen. A new Do City Manager arrives.

A designed dream is named and awakened. There is a giving in to joy, both in journey and in destination.

The unfolding of the huge dream has been informed and influenced by the "8-D test." The discernment leads to the design; the differentiation leads to the dropping, or the delegating, or the doing; the discipline leads to delight.

The process continues. We are free of the pouch of postponement. "I do not know" and "I do not understand" no longer dominate us. We give in to joy. We enjoy both clarity and commitment, both the

Give In To Joy

leaping and the landing! We decide to work more diligently on our thoughts. Then we choose to put our thoughts to work for us!

Giving In To Joy Made Easier

To set the stage for Chapter Seven (Think About The Thoughts You Think), and as a method of enhancing the force of this chapter (Give In To Joy), let us explore two specific thoughts that should bring you much joy. The first joy-thought is related to possibilities. The second joy-thought is related to perspective.

Possibilities Wear Camouflage

Possibilities do not always wear plain clothes. This is not a disturbing thought. It is a pleasant thought. Possibilities do not always have to look like Obvious Opportunity, Appropriate Avenue, or even Foreseeable Future.

You will miss many dream-possibilities if you deny yourself this fact. There is joy in thinking "camouflage." Dream opportunities often wear camouflage. They may hide in failure, adversity, insignificance, confusion, or routine. Dream-possibilities can often

THE KANGAROO FACTOR

be camouflaged as something else. The camouflage-uniform can conveniently be placed under three different "H" shelves. We can categorize these shelves as hardship, history, and hobby:

- Hardship – Adversity and confusion can create a hunger for calm and solution. Devise and build a dream that allows you to meet a need. Fill for others the void that you once felt in the midst of your own adversity. (Examples of how this could lead to dreams planned and dreams realized equal: childcare, repair work, and counseling.)
- History – Build on your life-experiences. (A speech teacher becomes a professional speaker. A ball player becomes a professional coach. A shopper becomes a professional shopper.)
- Hobby – Expand your hobby into a business if you so desire. (Cake decorating, gourmet cooking, working with crafts, and gardening might prove to be good examples.)

Possibilities do wear camouflage. Find reassurance in these thoughts:

Mystery, Misery, Or Mastery?

Dream Hinderers

Several years ago, I considered purchasing a business. I sought the advice of others before I totally immersed myself into my dream.

One of the persons with whom I talked was an expert in this particular field of work. Before I purchased the business, I thought it would be appropriate to spend some time with this particular expert.

We met. In both indirect and direct fashion, he dissuaded me from purchasing the business. I followed his advice.

Although I must take complete responsibility for my actions, I must also note that this same person later purchased the business that he advised me not to pursue. In retrospect, I wonder if he brought "purity of motive" into our time together.

For our purposes, there are three types of dream-hinderers:

- Competition
- Family Members
- Cheerleaders

THE KANGAROO FACTOR

Competition

Some will oppose your dream with the fear that it might jeopardize their agenda and their success. (This was perhaps illustrated in the preceding scenario listed under "Dream Hinderers.")

Competition can certainly create a crucible for jealousy, hidden motives, gossip, and dogged resistance.

This is not always the case. There are certainly exceptions to this rule. One phenomenal exception that I refer to so often is the National Speakers Association. It is comprised of almost 4,000 professional speakers, many of whom are vying for the same engagements. However, the members of this association equal the "best of the best" when it comes to authentically sharing with, and helping, each other.

In many instances, however, be leery of your competition when you seek to build your dream. Be aware of this: "Your competition's agenda may repeatedly rise above your dream-agenda."

Family Members

Discouragers often wear costumes that camouflage their spirit. One costume that discouragers often wear is that of "family member."

Mystery, Misery, Or Mastery?

You might automatically expect that your family members would occupy first place in the list that equals your cadre of dream-supporters. This will certainly, on occasion, prove to be the case. However, often this will prove to be very far from the truth.

For reasons that are too complex to address in a single book, family members may not always serve as allies to your dream. Family members, on occasion, may actually serve as your dream-enemy.

I mention this as a mode of warning: "Do not assume that family members will be first in line to support you and your dream."

Family members may eventually equal "dream-hinderers" for reasons of jealousy, incompetency, or lack of objectivity. Again, this will not always prove to be the case. Family members may certainly help bring vigor, virtue, and victory to you and your dream. The lesson here is this: "Exercise caution."

Cheerleaders

On first reading, the subheading "Cheerleaders" may appear as that which is in error. One, if inclined, could argue that cheerleaders stand apart from competitors and family members with hidden

THE KANGAROO FACTOR

agendas. Unfortunately, many so-called "cheerleaders" bring as much potential harm to you and your dream as do ruthless competitors and jealous family members.

There is of course one significant variable to be considered here. Whereas some competitors and some family members will seek to harm your dream by *intent*, some cheerleaders will impede your dream by *accident*.

For sure, some cheerleaders are intentionally violating any modicum of authenticity or integrity. They are simply throwing "good words" your way. In this case, the words are empty.

However, I lift up "cheerleaders" as potential "dream-hinderers", not because of any meanness or lack of integrity, but because of a naivety or lack of objectivity.

Earlier in *The Kangaroo Factor*, I referred to my tendency to elicit help from relatives, encouragers, neighbors, teachers, and students. Whenever I solicited the help of another, I received enthusiastic support. However, in a limited number of cases, the persons who cheered me with a magnificent level of intensity brought with them no discernment, no objectivity, no knowledge about my qualifications, and no valid insight into my dream.

Mystery, Misery, Or Mastery?

I should not have enlisted the help of such a cadre of inappropriate, and eventually ineffective, cheerleaders. When an error in judgment was made here, it was my responsibility. Again, a word of caution is essential. Choose your cheerleaders CAREFULLY.

Simply because someone cheers you and your dream on in a particular circumstance, does not mean you and your dream should be cheered in a particular circumstance. Please, let me encourage you to be certain that any cheerleading in relationship to your dream is based on the value and potential of your dream rather than the exuberance of cheerleaders who bring little more than naivety to task. Be very leery here. Refuse to be misled by a noisy cheerleader who yells encouragement from within a barrel called "naivety."

Mastering The Hinderers

The effective dreamer will isolate those persons who negatively impact his or her dream. In this instance, "isolation" refers to a "setting aside" that enables the dreamer to be less vulnerable to the negative influence of "dream-hinderers."

THE KANGAROO FACTOR

For sake of review, this sifting-process equals:

- Filtering the advice of competitors through the sieve of motive
- Weighing the influence of family members on an agenda-scale
- Monitoring the merit of cheerleaders through a gauge that monitors both objectivity and competency

Dream Helpers

Misery is eliminated, mystery is transcended, and mastery is celebrated when you encounter the grace and the courage to receive assistance from dream helpers. Your very capacity to receive help from others can have great impact on the realization of your dream.

You will be one significant step closer to dream mastery when you learn to categorize your dream helpers as:

- Those who talk
- Those who listen
- Those who confront
- Those who have written

Mystery, Misery, Or Mastery?

Those Who Talk

"Bounce" ideas off of another. Allow another to "talk back" to you. Again, it is crucial that you choose carefully the ones with whom you share your dream-ideas. Appropriate, well-targeted, and effective sharing should yield productive and profitable "talking" from those "in the know."

It is interesting to note that those "in the know" may actually prove to be persons from a mix that includes your competition, your family members, and your cheerleaders. Note afresh that there are exceptions to most every rule. You will often hear "effective," "helpful," and "authentic" talk coming from sources that equal your competition, your family members, and your cheerleaders. Remember our recurring mastery-theme here: "Let discernment be your guide."

Tape The Talk

You will be wise to tape, with the knowledge of your encouragers, their comments. The recording can be short and selective. Or you may prefer to record the entire session. An overwhelming majority of us make it a habit not to record those who uniquely inform and encourage us. We are missing a huge dream-mastery boat here.

Two of my ardent supporters are my father and my grandmother. The verb "are" rather than "were" is operative here because taped recordings enable me to continue benefiting from their words. (My father passed away at age 53 when I was 18; my grandmother passed away at age 103 when I was 43.) Granted, memory is a powerful gift. Its potency can be enhanced and expanded when you "tape the talk." Our moments are shortest at their longest, most delicate at their strongest. Do not waste the talk of your enthusiastic supporters. Tape it.

Your connections need not die through distance or death. They can live on, leading you toward dream-mastery, when you remember to tape the talk.

Those who talk to you about your dream can impact you and your dream immediately. If you are astute enough to tape the talk, then the benefit of that very single conversation may be multiplied as many times as you hear the talk you taped.

Those Who Listen

Not only do those who talk affect whether or not we master our dream, but those who listen can

Mystery, Misery, Or Mastery?

also impact both dream-journey and dream-destination. Those who listen to you can service your dream.

Thirty-plus years of study and observation have taught me that you and I possess a tremendous capacity to "self-start," "self-destruct," and "self-correct" in relationship to the mastery of our dream. Often, the miracle in relationship to all of this is the talk "we speak" – the talk "someone else merely hears." Those who listen to us talk about our dream contribute significantly to the mastering of our dream without saying a word. When a dreamer talks and another listens, a catalyst is created that can ignite significant dream-movement. In similar fashion, when a dreamer talks, and another listens, the dreamer can miraculously interpret the transparency of the listener. That transparency-interpretation serves as a magnificent rudder for future steps of total reversal, minor modification, or awesome acceleration.

Those Who Confront

It is both tempting and easy to fool yourself into believing that only those who affirm you care about you and your dream. This is certainly not always the case. Often, those persons who are willing to confront you in certain areas will prove to be

THE KANGAROO FACTOR

those who care the most about you and your dream-success.

With that said, may I once again simply remind you of that which you already know full well: "Often, those who care the most are those who care enough to suggest modifications."

This is certainly not a call to badger yourself with a composite of confrontation that is being hurled your way from every possible angle. It is, however, an invitation to learn and profit in relationship to your specific dream from those who care enough to challenge you and your thoughts in certain areas. It will be helpful to remember at this point that mastery, as it relates to your dream, has everything in the world to do with developing a positive relationship with those who care enough to challenge you. Postpone no longer an appropriate need to meet with those who are willing to care enough to question your presuppositions and even your precious plans.

Those Who Have Written

Your dream-helpers list must include authors and editors. How better can you expand and update your base of support? Your arsenal of dream-assistance

Mystery, Misery, Or Mastery?

can certainly feature a plethora of authors and editors who have written about dreaming and achieving.

Fully aware of this reality, I have included a substantial Recommended Reading List at the book's end. Inclusion in this list does not equal endorsement of a particular concept. Once again, you must exercise your choice-voice. I do, however, want you to have what I refer to as a massive "dreamer's smorgasbord" from which to choose.

I also want you to have the opportunity to benefit from some of my research, especially if you do not have the time or the inclination to pursue it in its largest context. Therefore, I want to highlight three entries from the Recommended Reading List. I, in no way, want to slight the other entries. Specifically, I want to illustrate how a particular author or editor can function as your dream-helper. Bibliographical data on each entry will be included in the Recommended Reading List beginning on page 267.

THE KANGAROO FACTOR

All In One Room

How would you like to bring many of the world's greatest dreamers into a single room? How would you like to benefit from their insights?

Peter Krass, editor of *The Book Of Entrepreneur's Wisdom – Classic Writing By Legendary Entrepreneurs*, has brought these great dreamers into one room, or one book. Your potential for benefiting from the powerful writings of these entrepreneurs is awesome. I wish there had been a book precisely like this decades ago.

I feel it inappropriate to list the names of all of those persons who are featured in this marvelous book. It will be helpful, however, for you to appreciate the scope of this massive assortment of dreamers. Therefore, I will list a significant number of those whose writings are shared. I encourage you to sample enough of the smorgasbord offerings so as to experience the fullness that they might bring to your dream.

The Book of Entrepreneur's Wisdom – Classic Writing By Legendary Entrepreneurs, as edited by Peter Krass, features an impressive cast of diverse dreamers and achievers including:

Mystery, Misery, Or Mastery?

Lillian Vernon
Harvey S. Firestone
Walley Amos
Barry Diller
Warren Avis
Andrew Carnegie
Conrad Hilton
Dave Thomas
J.C. Penney

Michael S. Dell
Benjamin Franklin
Clarence Birdseye
P.T. Barnum
Colonel Harland Sanders
Samuel Goldwyn
Henry Ford
Victor Kiam
Marquis M. Converse

Benefit from this book. It will make it possible for you to bring these effective dreamers into the same book-room with you.

From All Over The World

It is often my pleasure to deliver the baccalaureate message to graduating seniors. On occasion, the message gifts me with the opportunity to meet the valedictorian, the salutatorian, and the senior class president. In other instances, I benefit from reading about those who lead their class academically (valedictorian and salutatorian) and technically (class president).

My observation, based on what I have seen and what I have read, is worthy of notation. The

THE KANGAROO FACTOR

percentage of immigrants who have graduated at the top of their class, or near the top of their class, is remarkable. If you were to take the senior classes from throughout America and analyze them, you would discover that a number of these classes have elected class presidents who came to America from another country.

One could argue that these persons, coming to America from all over the world, have the odds stacked against them. In many instances they must learn a second language and absorb a new culture, even as they work before and after school. People like me, persons who struggle with dream-mastery, can learn a great deal from people like them, their parents, and their grandparents.

With this "from all over the world" theme as our current backdrop, it is now my pleasure to lift up for your consideration a book by a fellow speaker and author. Marcia Steele's *Making It In America – What Immigrants Know and Americans Have Forgotten* touches the issue that I am addressing here.

Her book affirms all Americans who dare to pursue dream-mastery. It is loaded with help for you and your dream. Her work equals what I would describe as a candid and personal guide for all dreamers. In *Making It In America*, Marcia A. Steele

Mystery, Misery, Or Mastery?

writes: "One of the biggest challenges facing us in America today is not global competition or technology, but rather complacency and fear! Half of us are complacent with the status quo and the other half live in fear of losing the status quo."

This dream-helper's book is loaded with numerous examples of immigrants from different nations and different walks of life who have experienced dream-mastery. It can certainly "fire your imagination."

From A Life Of Business To The Business Of Life

The preceding sub-heading is actually the sub-title for the book I now highlight. The lead title for this work is *Kiss Yourself Hello!* It challenges each dreamer to add "salt 'n pepper" to their lives in spite of their age.

When I challenge you to ponder this particular book, I recognize that I am certainly not alone. Those persons who have written favorably about Phil Parker's *Kiss Yourself Hello!* include: Les Brown, Fran Tarkenton, Nido R. Qubein, and Raleigh Pinskey.

THE KANGAROO FACTOR

Gift yourself with a copy of *Kiss Yourself Hello! From A Life Of Business To The Business Of Life* by Phil Parker. Allow Phil's insight to assist you as you sojourn toward dream-mastery. Benefit from Phil as he challenges you to: "Re-visit your past, study the present, build your dreams, and create your future."

Brain Food

Before we proceed, let me encourage you to think of a book as dream food, brain food, seizing food. If you cooperate with it, the appropriate book can enable you to leap from your pouch of postponement and land in the world of planned dreams and realized dreams.

The preceding sentence holds within it two crucial words to our thinking: "cooperate" and "appropriate." Be very selective in both your thinking and in your acting. Choose to read books that are appropriate to your internal mandates. When the appropriateness (integrity) test is passed, then cooperate with the portions of the book that authentically and effectively support your personhood. Be very careful here. The books you choose to read may well affect you and your dream!

Think About The Thoughts You Think

When Two Equal All The Difference In The World

If you sincerely want to give in to joy during dream-journey and dream-destination, then you must significantly ponder the thoughts you think in relationship to:

1) Postponement
2) Pursuit

The thoughts you think, and the very words you pronounce to yourself and to others, will strongly influence the eventual outcome.

A view from the postponement-pouch is always a limited view. By the very nature of location, it is impossible to look all around you. The "outside-view" is limited as long as you choose to remain in your postponement-pouch.

If you are constantly dwelling on "downbeat" words (anxiety, bleak, boredom, chore, dissatisfaction, failure, frustrated, impossible, inadequate, incapable, unable, and uncertain), and the numerous other words listed under column one (postponement), then you are stacking the odds against yourself.

THE KANGAROO FACTOR

To repeatedly postpone pouch-departure is to risk destruction of your dream. Your risk factor will be significantly greater if you constantly think and speak "postponement-words."

However, if you persistently think and speak upbeat words (bright, excitement, conscientious, choice, hope, enjoy, possible, positive, opportunity, progress, confident), and the numerous other "pursuit-words" as expressed in column two, then you are stacking the odds in your favor.

A meaningful dream-journey and a successful dream-realization have everything in the world to do with outlook. Outlook crystallizes for us the two factors that make a world of difference: Postponement or Pursuit. The manner in which your mind allows you to marry outlook to preparation will seriously impact, as a deciding factor, whether or not you cling to the postponement-pouch.

Ultimately, "you" do make all the difference in the world. What will it be for you? Will it be postponement and procrastination? Or will it be pursuit and an effective leaping and landing activity? In the final analysis, the answer to those questions is related to the thoughts you think and the very words you speak.

Think About The Thoughts You Think

Think About The Thoughts You Think

We think about the clothes we wear,
About every gift we choose to share,
Even of our eyes – and why they blink,
But seldom do we think about the thoughts we think.

We think, from time to time, about the words we say,
And every game on rainy day we might play,
Even of others – and wonder what they think,
But seldom do we think about the thoughts we think.

Sad it is that this mind, spinning miles a minute,
Finds little time to study our thoughts within it,
To target a thought – to catch and weigh and ponder,
To study thought's source and strength, and to wonder.

We need not stay the way we are.
Truth be known, we may have already come far.
Before moment will once again blink,
We can indeed think about the thoughts we think.

Stephen M. Gower
Winter 2000

CHAPTER 8

Tell Your Past Where To Go

I have made a beautiful discovery during the winter of 2000. For many years, I have been told that the yellow finch was a delightful bird to observe. Up until now, I have been denied the opportunity to see for myself. However, this year, our backyard is inundated with that darling bird, the yellow finch. As far as I am concerned, and the good Lord willing, I will never experience again the void of the playful yellow finch during the winter. In effect, I have told my yellow finch-less past where to go. I told it to go away. I have stopped buying junk-seed, the seed that will not

THE KANGAROO FACTOR

attract the yellow finch. I now buy the good stuff, the sunflower and thistle stuff.

Now, for sure, telling one's past, both the historical past and the hysterical past, to go away is not always necessary. It is not always possible. It is not even always good! However, sometimes it is necessary, sometimes it is very good, to tell parts of our past where to go.

When I speak of "our past" in this fashion, I refer to the very thoughts it engenders. The thoughts our past creates can inspire us, encourage us, teach us, warn us, and befriend us. But our past can also irritate us. It can interrupt our dream-growth. It can cause us to "rest on our laurels." It can torture us. It can wear us down; it can belittle us.

It will be prudent for you to be cautious and selective as you exercise the challenge of telling your past where to go. You will not want to tell all of it to "go away." You will want to keep some of it around, and even within you. You will want to tell some of it to "stay." I have decided that those past, yellow finch-less winters are winters that I want to go away. I do not want them around anymore. Accordingly, I will buy no more junk seed. I will buy the good stuff. I plan to have enough sunflower and thistle around to assure that my yellow finch-less past is around no more. That past I have told to go away.

Tell Your Past Where To Go

Sometimes You Say, "Go Away"

On a more serious note, I repeatedly am trying to tell the past of a skinny, selfish, stubborn, smart aleck Stephen where to go. I have learned enough from it. To perpetually dwell on it now would not only equal an unnecessary detour. It would also lead to wasted moments and lost energy. I have told that self-debasing past where to go. I have told it to go away. And, most of the time, it listens.

I have something to say to the past that includes the classes I cut and the tests I tried to "finesse" rather than prepare for on a regular basis. I want to shout something to that past of my life centered upon the time when I relentlessly teased my sister and made life difficult for my mother. To those past moments I shout, "Go away; stop hounding me. I have heard what you have been saying to me. I have changed. Now go away. For good."

Other Times You Say, "Stay"

However, I certainly could never tell my "grandmother Weezie past" to go away. I would not want to do that, nor should I do that. The Weezie-part of my past services me to this very day. Without

THE KANGAROO FACTOR

attempting to live in a make-believe world, but rightfully respecting my grandmother, when I tell that past where to go, I say, "Stay – please stay."

Yes, there is a past in each of us that needs to be told where to go (away). That past is denying us big dreams. That past is robbing us of big thoughts. That past is the bandit that steals moments away from us, the very moments we should be seizing.

There is also a past to be valued. Not merely for its teaching-value or its caution-value, but also for its core-value. This past we value for its goodness, its very merit. We also need to tell this past where to go (stay).

Accordingly, I want the good and solid and helpful part of my past to hang around in my memory: when God intervened, when Mom and Dad stepped in time and again, when Weezie worked her wonders, when my wife encouraged me.

I cannot tell your past where to go. Of course, that is up to you. I will state this, however. You will never be awake and alert enough to seize your crucial-possibility moments as long as your negative, past-based thoughts dominate your thinking. Do not allow your mind to mold and hold nothing but negative, past-based thoughts.

Tell Your Past Where To Go

> **You will never dream your biggest dreams as long as your negative, past-based thoughts DOMINATE your thinking.**

In similar fashion, you will never be awake and alert enough to seize your vital possibility moments as long as you refuse to allow your positive, past-based thoughts to serve you. Your reservoir of positive, past-based thoughts is a powerhouse arsenal that awaits your invitation.

> **You will never dream your biggest dreams as long as you refuse to allow your positive, past-based thoughts to SERVE you.**

This very concept applies not only to thoughts related to the past. It also applies to thoughts related to the present – and the future. This "present and future" aspect of one's thought-life is so important that it mandates our attention in Chapters Nine and Ten.

THE KANGAROO FACTOR

Before we proceed, however, please allow me to give some names and brief descriptions to the faces of negative, past-based thoughts, and to the faces of positive, past-based thoughts. And as you read these names and brief descriptions, please hold these three statements in center-place of your head and your heart:

1) You can minimize, or eliminate, the power of negative, past-based thoughts over you.
2) You can enhance, or expand, the power of positive, past-based thoughts over you.
3) In each instance you locate, isolate, and relocate a particular set of thoughts.

The Negative, Past-Based Thoughts

Complaining

- Launched out from self-pity
- A self-induced misery
- A woeful, even pathetic, lamenting and whining
- A get-back-at-them mentality
- Must be thrown away

Tell Your Past Where To Go

Revenge

- Does you more harm than them
- Starves you of energy
- Targets "them," not "your dream"
- Must be thrown away

Guilt

- "Guilt" often equals one's own worst enemy.
- "I am too bad to be good, too bad to do this."
- Faith equals the answer– perhaps redirection.
- Excessive guilt must be thrown away. (On occasion, however, we do feel guilty, because we should feel guilty.)

The Positive, Past-Based Thoughts

Compassion

- Remembrances of times past when you lost yourself for others
- Your best "self" resurfacing in other-centered focusing
- Hold this within you.

THE KANGAROO FACTOR

Respect

- People we respect can be mirrored within our hearts and out from our spirit.
- Hold this within you.

Growth

- Any past models of growth that you previously experienced should excite and encourage you.
- Look to your positive experiences in sports, in church, in school, in relationships.
- Hold this within you.

> **You can MINIMIZE, or ELIMINATE, the power of negative, past-based thoughts over you. You can ENHANCE, or EXPAND, the power of positive, past-based thoughts over you.**

Retention Or Release

The issue of your past, whether it helps or hurts, whether it should be retained within your mind

Tell Your Past Where To Go

and spirit, or released from you mind and spirit, is of course up to you. And once again, your ability to pass the first D (discernment) in our "8-D Test" is crucial. You must maximize your ability to discern the portion of your negative past that hounds you from the portion of your positive past that helps you. And you must move on, with professional help if necessary.

You must locate a thought, isolate and examine the thought, and then relocate the thought or family of thoughts. In simple terms, your thought-relocator place equals either a "go-away place" or a "stay place."

Naturally, to the extent that it is possible, you want to tell your hounding, negative, past-based thoughts where to go (away). In the same vein, you want to tell your helpful, positive, past thoughts where to go (stay).

You want to target your thoughts. To the extent that it is possible for you, you want to isolate and "take aim" at any hounding, negative thoughts related to your past. You want to aim at them, hit bull's eye, and move on. Do not allow those hounding, negative thoughts based on your past to hang around and harm you. Tell them where to go (away)!

THE KANGAROO FACTOR

You also want to target any positive thoughts arriving out of your past. Target them in such a fashion as to allow them to resurface. Actually invite them to become an encouraging part of your giving in to joy! Invite them to assist you in your dreaming big, your thinking big, and your seizing and mastering your moments! (Example: I am repeatedly allowing thoughts of my encouraging "You can do it, Stephen" grandmother to resurface within my head and heart.)

Remember the key here lies within your capacity to discern. In relationship to the thoughts out of your past, you ask yourself two questions: Which thoughts should I *release*? Which thoughts should I *retain*? In each case, you locate, isolate and examine, and relocate.

The appropriate retention and release of thoughts will inform and influence your capacity to leap away from your postponement-pouch and your tendency to procrastinate. Balancing release with retention, you can dream big, think big, and seize your moments.

> **To RELEASE or to RETAIN?**
> **That is the crucial issue.**

Tell Your Past Where To Go

Thought-Life Targeting

In the next two chapters, as we continue to explore the entire issue of thought-life targeting, we will notice two tremendous concepts at play:

1) There is a significant overlapping, or intertwining, between your thought-life as it involves your past, and your thought-life as it relates to your present and your future.
2) Whatever your past thought-life, and whatever your present and future thought-life, you do not have to stay the way you are!

Past Performance

This book is being written in the winter of the year 2000. Tax time is just around the corner. I, along with millions of you, will hurriedly study a plethora of mutual fund prospectus-booklets in order to ascertain where to place this year's retirement funds.

I must admit that I am repeatedly intrigued by a common-denominator factor on each prospectus. Although the actual historical rates of return will vary, most funds will list one, three, five, even ten-year

THE KANGAROO FACTOR

rates of return. Normally, these lists indicate returns that are at least somewhat favorable.

However, and here is the common-denominator-factor clincher, there is normally an asterisk adjacent to the ten-year rate of return. That asterisk will then lead you to another asterisk placed near the bottom of the page. It will read quite vividly: "Past performance is not indicative of future results."

I have reminded numerous audiences of a phenomenal reality: "When it comes to investing, the asterisk is a caution." Simply because rates of return were once good does not guarantee that they will always be good. However, "When it comes to human growth, to holding true to the discipline of mastery, this asterisk is not a caution. It is a mighty challenge." This must become the center of your giving in to joy: "PAST PERFORMANCE IS NOT INDICATIVE OF YOUR FUTURE RESULTS."

Tell your negative, past-based thoughts where to go. Tell them to go away. Tell your positive, past-based thoughts where to go. Tell them to stay. By minimizing or eliminating the hurt of the negative past, and by duplicating or expanding the benefit of the positive past, you can move past procrastination toward productivity.

Tell Your Past Where To Go

Let me encourage you. Wherever you are in your life, remember this: "You do not have to stay the way you are. Past performance is definitely not indicative of your future results! You possess the awesome power to become. You need not be confined to the pouch of postponement. You can leap!"

> **You do not have to stay the way you are. Past performance is definitely not indicative of your future results! You possess the awesome POWER TO BECOME!**

Seed-Sifting

Target your thoughts. Change your thinking environment so that it works for you, not against you. Locate, isolate and examine, and relocate any thought that is harmful. Help it go away. Train yourself to think positively.

Chunk years into months, months into weeks, weeks into days, days into hours, and hours into minutes. If you cannot think positively for a full hour, then give your head and heart to thinking positively for fifteen minutes. As you celebrate the little

THE KANGAROO FACTOR

chunks of thought-success, you will find yourself positioned for larger chunks.

Locate, isolate and examine, and relocate any thought that is positive. Help it to stay. Again, train yourself to think positively.

Build upon your positive thoughts. Allow one family of positive thoughts to invite other families of positive thoughts. Create a contagion of positive thoughts. Celebrate the accumulation.

Sift your thought-seeds. Examine and sort them. Examine them afresh.

Do you want your winters blessed with the bird named the yellow finch? Then tell your yellow finch-less past where to go (away). Secure for yourself sunflower and thistle seed.

If you have a huge bag of old seed, and most of us do, sift through it. Throw away the old, negative, "yellow finch-less" seed. Sort out the good stuff, the sunflower seed and the thistle seed. Refuse to expect the sorting to reach completion in one big event. Think "process."

Throw away the negative junk-stuff. Throw away the complaining and the pitying, the revenge and the self-draining, the guilt and the remorse, the incessant "not knowing." Examine closely your old bag of negative seed. See it for what it is. View it as

Tell Your Past Where To Go

destructive to your dream. Understand it as that which equals a wasting of your time. Perceive it as procrastination in disguise.

Hold on to seeds of commitment, positive attitude, preparation, seeds of respect, and seeds of growth. See them for what they are. Respect them as constructive in relationship to your dream. Ponder them as time well spent. Value them as potential being unleashed.

Look into your history. Separate, to the best of your ability, the negative from the positive. Using professional help if necessary, sift through the seeds that equal your past. You will tell them where to go. You will tell some to go away. You will tell others to stay. Remember, your winters, springs, summers, and falls need not stay the way they are! You can indeed leap into an exciting world of big dreams, big thoughts, moments mastered.

Your dream-quotient has everything in the world to do with the way you handle your thoughts. Do they control you or do you control them?

CHAPTER 9

Throw Your Negative Thoughts In The Dump

He is as different from me as up is from down, as day is from night, as dry is from wet. However, for some reason, we hit it off. I always enjoy seeing him – and being with him. He is a fine man. I see him an average of once a week.

He runs our county dumpsite. It has to be the cleanest dumpsite in the country. Just last week he chastised me for dropping garbage on the concrete adjacent to his huge bins. After I cleaned up my mess

THE KANGAROO FACTOR

and cranked Old Blue, my '77 Chevy pickup, I heard him say what he always says: "Thanks for your business. You come back now." However, it is not his farewell comments that linger in my mind right now. It is the comments he utters upon my arrival. For more than five years, our initial conversation has unfolded like this:

>Him: "Where are we headed next?"
>Me: "Seattle, then San Francisco – (whatever)"
>Him: "Well, I'm ready to go with you."
>Me: "Great, let's do it."
>Him: "Now, there will be no flying, will there?"
>Me: "Of course, that's the only way."
>Him: "Not me, man. You'll never get me up there."
>Me: "Why not?"
>Him: "No way. It might fall down in a hurry."
>Me: "Well, I'll miss you."
>Him: "Oh, I'll be with you. I'll just be down here, looking up. As a matter of fact I think I saw you up there last week."

Throw Your Negative Thoughts In The Dump

Same stanza, same chorus. For five years now. He is definitely my buddy. But I do not go to the dump just to see him. Neither do I go to the dumpsite out of necessity. Someone else could go. Strange as it may sound, I like going to the dump.

You Can Learn A Lot At A Dump

This section of our time together is a testimonial to the art of discarding. It states, with unabashed conviction, that there can be genius in casting-aside, a brilliance in throwing-out. There can be wisdom in rejecting this or that. There can be a benefit in leaving the postponement-pouch at the dump.

My visits to the county-dump vigorously remind me that it is not always wisest to retain. It is not always beneficial to clutch, not always prudent to keep in hand.

My times at the county-dump say to me: "Sometimes it is best to let loose and let go." It is almost as if those huge dump-bins bellow out to me: "Here is where you are to place your dirty, old stuff, your jagged tin cans, your rotten scraps."

THE KANGAROO FACTOR

The Thought-Dumpsite

I encourage you to visualize a dumpsite that has placed on its outside a huge welcome sign for you. Once you move beyond that sign on to the dumpsite grounds, imagine seeing instructions similar to the following:

- Drop your old postponement-pouch here.
- Here is a bin named Torture Thought. Use it.
- Here is a bin named Fear Thought. Use it.
- Here is a bin named Comparison Thought. Use it.

> **The THOUGHT-DUMPSITE can equal a VERY GOOD place.**

If you believe that there are negative thoughts and positive thoughts and that both will impact your dream, you may be asking yourself two questions about your thoughts:

- Who makes my thoughts for me?
- Who determines where my thoughts go?

Throw Your Negative Thoughts In The Dump

You Equal The Answers

Of course, "you" are the answers to both questions. Ultimately, you must take responsibility for the thoughts you make, both negative and positive. And ultimately, you must take responsibility for where you place your thoughts, both negative and positive. In both instances, thought-construction and thought-placement, you make the choices. You must listen to your own choice-voice. You are in charge of thought-construction; you are in charge of thought-placement! You cannot assign these duties to someone else.

**You are in charge of THOUGHT-CONSTRUCTION!
You are in charge of THOUGHT-PLACEMENT!**

Chapter Ten will address our positive thought-construction and our positive thought-placement. In this chapter, we have the challenge of examining negative thought-construction and negative thought-placement.

THE KANGAROO FACTOR

Earlier we encountered three Dream Blocks that are each related to negative thoughts: torture, fear, and comparison. Let us now give each one a name:

- The Torture Tool
- The Fear Fabricator
- The Comparison Creator

The Torture Tool

I remain amazed at the things we do to ourselves with our minds. We take something that is marvelous and wonderful. We turn it into something else: The Torture Tool!

This tool does not build; it tears down, perpetually so. This tool is not constructive in nature; it is destructive by nature, dramatically so.

When our mind chooses to construct and retain negative thoughts, we have in effect created a Torture Tool. The Torture Tool cares nothing about naming a dream, about awakening a dream, about giving in to joy. Indeed, it wants to block and stop the dream. It loves the pouch of postponement

As a college professor for more than a decade, I watched The Torture Tool work its havoc on young

Throw Your Negative Thoughts In The Dump

minds. As an observer of the corporate culture for more than a quarter of a century, I have viewed The Torture Tool play its role of dream-spoiler. I have heard, with shocking clarity, persons most blessed shout:

- "No."
- "Not me."
- "I am not good enough."
- "I am not smart enough."
- "I cannot do this."
- "Never."
- "Impossible."
- "I am making no difference."
- "What I am doing here is no good."
- "I am not good."
- "It will never work."
- "It will be a waste of time."
- "It is too big for me to tackle."
- "It is too important for me to attempt it."

This negative babble, this concoction of self-debasing verbiage, can wrestle a person into submission, denying that person of joyful dream-journey. It can rob him or her of dream-leaping and dream-landing.

THE KANGAROO FACTOR

There Is An Antidote

The antidote to the poison administered by The Torture Tool reveals itself in a particular discipline: The Discipline Of Mastery. There is a specific expertise available to you. It equals this very discipline. The exciting news is this: You already have it within you. We will explore this reality in Part Four, "Seize Your Moment".

For now, let me make it clear that the medicine for combating the tool that administers torture is already within you. You already possess, deep inside you, a tool that is far superior to The Torture Tool. This superior tool is waiting for you to seize it – not from without, but from within yourself. And once you do seize it, once you utilize the discipline that equals mastery, you find the wisdom and the strength to take your negative thoughts where they belong – to the dump. You will learn more about this tool, this very Discipline Of Mastery Tool, in Chapter Twelve. At this point, let me simply describe this tool as that which effectively counters negative, internal babble. It defeats excessive pouch-talk. It overcomes tiny-step talk. It will actually enable you to talk positively, purposefully, and profitably to yourself.

Throw Your Negative Thoughts In The Dump

When you think about the thoughts you think, you will discover many thoughts forged by The Torture Tool. Take those thoughts to the dump. Certainly, The Torture Tool is not the only force that creates those nasty, negative thoughts that should be taken to the dump. For our purposes, and as stated earlier, there are at least two other tools that work to manufacture negative thoughts, counter-productive thoughts, Could City thoughts, and dream-block thoughts. One tool equals The Fear Fabricator. The other tool equals The Comparison Creator.

The Fear Fabricator

"Fabricate" is a strong word here. But it gifts us with restatement and reinforcement.

This is certainly no superficial avoidance of the reality that there are those things worth fearing, even circumstances worth fearing. However, in this section, we want to address the thoughts of fear that we inappropriately fabricate. With Fear Fabricator in hand, we make negative thoughts – thoughts that look and sound like the following:

- "I might fail. I will be embarrassed."
- "I might succeed. That will be new for me. I will be scared."

THE KANGAROO FACTOR

- "If I do succeed, what will they expect of me next? Even more?"

For the most part these negative thoughts are predominately forged by The Fear Fabricator. They need to be examined closely. I can think of situations that would justify dumping each of these statements into the waste dump.

Our Fear Fabricator manufactures two different genres of fear:

- Fear of failure (embarrassment-rooted)
- Fear of success (expectation-rooted)

Fear Of Failure
Embarrassment-Rooted

If our fear of failing is rooted in a concern that we might be embarrassed by a certain turn of events, we must examine the attention we are giving to "what others might think." When "what others might think" rules over the very thoughts we think, we are giving others a tremendous amount of power over us. We acquiesce (give in) to others a tremendous amount of power over our very dreams.

Throw Your Negative Thoughts In The Dump

Now, there is nothing wrong with asking for second and third opinions. Sometimes this is not only important, it is necessary. That is not the issue I address here. I am referring to our very dream situations that we allow to be controlled, deterred, or delayed because we feel we might be embarrassed if we fail. When we allow our dreams to be delayed because we fear possible embarrassment-rooted failure, we are allowing others to determine how we feel about ourselves. This is wrong. It gives others much more power over us than they deserve.

Think twice before you surrender to a fear of failure grounded in potential embarrassment. See this for what it is. It is your willingness to allow others to determine how you feel about yourself. Take charge here. Remember something very crucial: "Ultimately, others will not determine how you feel about yourself unless you cooperate with them." Others will not possess power over your feelings unless you give it to them.

Remember something very crucial: "Ultimately, others will not determine how you feel about yourself unless you COOPERATE with them."

THE KANGAROO FACTOR

Do not manufacture within yourself a fear of failure that hinges on what others think. Listen to your own highest and best choice voice.

Fear Of Success Expectation-Rooted

As I address the issue of fear of success in presentations, and as I write about it, I am sure it is often greeted with a deep surprise. It is as if another is asking: "Why in the world would I be afraid of success? I want success. That is why I am attending this seminar or reading this book."

Certainly, the fear of success can be very complex. It can be deep-rooted. For our purposes, it will be appropriate to address two common explanations of this fabricated fear, often labeled "fear of success":

- "Realization of my dream, as much as I think I want it, would be new territory. It would be a success I have never experienced before. I always feel very awkward around the 'new.' I expect that I will not handle the 'new' very well."

Throw Your Negative Thoughts In The Dump

- "If I succeed, I am afraid others will expect success to be piled upon success. I am afraid I might be held to a much higher level of accountability simply because I have succeeded once. I do not want that to happen, but I expect that to happen if I succeed."

Ultimately, we are the very ones who make and mold our own fear of success. Accordingly, we must personally apply our own What? Why? How? System to our situation:

- What am I fearing here?
- Why does this fear have power over me?
- How can I respond?

On occasion, mentoring and perhaps even professional help may be necessary. However, at this point, let us remember the following:

- The thoughts we think related to fear of success can deter and delay and even block the dream.
- There is an appropriate place for these inappropriate thoughts. It is called "the dump."

THE KANGAROO FACTOR

- It is much better to feel awkward about the exciting and the new than it is to feel awkward about the boring, the meaninglessness, and the stagnant. Total "awkwardlessness" is an illusion.

> **It is much better to feel awkward about the EXCITING and the NEW than it is to feel awkward about the BORING, the MEANINGLESSNESS, and the STAGNANT.**

If you are fabricating a fear that calls itself fear of success, and if that fear rises out of the awkwardness that equals "an exciting new," read and ponder the following paragraph. If your fear of success is based on the expectations that others would have of you, then read and ponder the following paragraph.

You are called to be your best self, not your perfect self. You are called to be a growing self. Growth often travels by the way of the new, even the "successful new." It can be meaningful, even magnificent. It can be so meaningful and magnificent that it would be a shame for it to be marred by a fear of success. Do not ground your dreams because you

Throw Your Negative Thoughts In The Dump

fear the "new world" your success might create. Do not ground your dreams because others might expect more and more of you. Pray. Be true to Him and to your potential. Remember, there will be times when an expectation-based fear of success should be taken to the dump.

Keep things in perspective. Refuse to allow an inappropriate fear to keep you bound in the pouch.

> Your challenge is to be your BEST SELF, not your PERFECT SELF.

The Comparison Creator

Normally, when we think of creativity, we think of it in positive terms. When one describes another as being a "creative" person, that one is normally complimenting the other. Normally, creativity is associated with "the positive."

Here, however, as fear expresses itself afresh, something very negative is being created. A nagging and nauseating "comparing" has been born. There is the creation of The Horrible Composite. It is manufactured by The Comparison Creator run wild.

THE KANGAROO FACTOR

It is "horrible" because we use it to block away any hint of a dream. We employ it to destroy our named and awakened dream. It is a "composite" because it is a mixture. It is a conscious gathering of the best of everyone else.

For sure, some of us compare ourselves to another salesperson, another teacher, another student, another leader, another parent, another team member. We compare and we moan: "I'll never do this as well as him or her." As a result of our individual comparing, one-to-one, we measure ourselves. We fall short. We lose our momentum.

The Horrible Composite, however, is much more destructive than an individual comparing of one-to-one. Through The Horrible Composite, we do not compare ourselves to one, a perceived superior one. We compare ourselves to many, to the accumulated best of everyone else.

The "Horrible Composite thoughts" we think harm us. They dumbfound, dissuade, and defeat. They need to be taken to the dump. Do not stack the odds against yourself by infesting your mind with thoughts that emerge out from this Horrible Composite. Your barometer is your best self, not the composite of everyone else's best self. You are accountable for your talents, not everyone else's

Throw Your Negative Thoughts In The Dump

talents. Your dream's departure and arrival is to be steered by your God-given best, not the best of everyone else.

> **Your barometer is your BEST SELF, not THE HORRIBLE COMPOSITE of everyone else's best self.**

When you constantly gauge your potential on their performance level, when you repeatedly create and view a collage of every one else's superior achievement, you set yourself up for perpetual discouragement.

Focus on your best. Concentrate on your dream. Refuse to be distracted by the picture you drew, the picture that you unfortunately continue to flash in front of your head and heart, the picture of everyone else's best. Throw it away. Discard it. Tell it where to go. Take it to the dump.

This Will Help

Do not focus on reaching or exceeding the combined best of everyone else (an impossible feat

THE KANGAROO FACTOR

for any one of us). Focus on recognizing, and even rewarding, your best steps:

- Chunk your own dream down into little steps.
- Choose to focus your energy on your best small steps, not everyone else's best big steps.
- Categorize your small steps into your own composite. Give so much of your mind to a composite of your crucial, small steps that there is little space for the counter-productive thoughts associated with the total of everyone else's best.
- Celebrate incremental finishedness. We will visit this issue more in depth in Part Four, "Seize The Moment." For now, let me simply, but strongly, encourage you to reward yourself when you complete any small-step phase of your dream.

This chunking down, categorizing, and celebrating of incremental finishedness will help you replace The Horrible Composite, not with a void that will never be strong enough to do the job, but with your own system for focusing on your best. Again, it

Throw Your Negative Thoughts In The Dump

is not enough to *remove* The Horrible Composite. The Horrible Composite must be *replaced* with Cyclical Celebration.

When you choose to celebrate incremental finishedness rather than be deterred by The Horrible Composite, you stack the odds in your favor. If you chunk your progress down to its simplest core, and if you follow *The Kangaroo Factor* faithfully, there should always be something to celebrate. The cycle should never end. This does not mean there will be no detours. It simply is an invitation to look for the positive.

There Is Always Room

My friend at the dump has never told me to go home before I threw the garbage in his bins. He has always found room in the dump for my stuff.

There is always room in the dump for your negative thoughts. In particular, there is a space there for your Torture Tool. There is a spot there for your Fear Fabricator. There is a section there for your Comparison Creator. The dump is calling for your postponement-pouch.

THE KANGAROO FACTOR

> **There is ALWAYS ROOM for your negative thoughts in the dump!**

It is pack-up time. It is head-to-the-dump time. What do you need to take with you?

- Your Torture Tool (negative self-talk rooted)
- Your Fear Fabricator (embarrassment and expectation rooted)
- Your Comparison Creator (Horrible Composite rooted)
- Your Postponement-Pouch (the sum of all of the above)

Remember, there is always room for this stuff in the dump! Take it there!!

CHAPTER 10

Take Your Positive Thoughts To The Bank

I saw him today – about eighty years old – tall, lanky, a slight stoop. For the past several years, he has greeted me with a "howdy" and a special spirit. It has not always been smooth sailing between us. The fault was mine.

Many years ago, I amused Northeast Georgia and portions of the Western Carolinas by serving as color commentator for our high school football broadcasts on Friday nights. I was not very good. I am not even sure I was tolerable. But, in spite of

THE KANGAROO FACTOR

myself, what I did became a tradition that lasted almost fifteen years.

One Saturday morning, mid-season, I ran into this gentleman after the previous Friday night's game. Our conversation went something like this:

"You know the field goal holder has a name, too."

"Excuse me?"

"The field goal holder! Every time a field goal is made, you mention the kicker's name – but you never mention the holder's name."

He was right. I was wrong. One of his relatives was the field goal holder, an outstanding athlete, a tremendous young man. I was embarrassed. I apologized and self-corrected. He forgave. All is well.

Just as it is never enough to have a strong field goal kicker, just as you must have a strong and steady holder, it is never enough to merely take your negative thoughts to the dump. You must also replace your negative thoughts with positive thoughts. Then you must take your positive thoughts to the bank so that they can grow and work for you.

There were two concepts that surfaced in our previous chapter that must resurface here:

Take Your Positive Thoughts To The Bank

- The mind does not hold void or vacuum; it holds thoughts.
- Any mixture of negative thoughts (Torture Tool thoughts, Fear Fabricator thoughts, Comparison Creator thoughts) must be replaced – not merely removed.

Good For Something

Your mind is not designed to be "good for nothing." It is not manufactured to hold "void" or "vacuum" or "emptiness." Neither is your mind designed for "the bad." It is not built to be a house that holds "hurt," "harm," "dream destruction," or "negative self-talk."

Your mind is designed for good. And it is "good for something!" It is good for "many somethings." It is very good for dreaming, for servicing, for reflecting, for planning, for being, for doing, for leaping, and for landing.

Your mind is a "MOLD AND HOLD" vessel.

THE KANGAROO FACTOR

Your mind, and the very thoughts you think, can enable you to "help yourself to success." Your mind can help you release the "marvelous you" that is already there within you. Your mind can help you sculpt your best. It can help you be your best! It can help you do your best!

Your mind can mold wonderful ideas. It can hold those ideas so the inventory is fresh, ready, and powerful. Your mind is good for your dream!

Replacement Is The Key

If your mind is to do its good, then you must do something good. If your mind is to help you dream big, think big, and seize the moment, then you must take appropriate steps. If your mind is to enable you to "help yourself to success," if it is to help you pursue the discipline of mastery, then you need to do two things:

- Strive to remove negative thoughts.
- Seek to replace them with positive thoughts.

Step one will do you no good unless you follow it quickly with step two. Remember, the mind does not hold "nothing." It does hold "something."

Take Your Positive Thoughts To The Bank

It will hold negative thoughts. Or it will hold positive thoughts. Quite likely, it will hold a combination of both.

Naturally, your aim is to seek to minimize or eliminate negative thoughts and to duplicate or enhance positive thoughts. Complete elimination of negative thoughts will rarely occur. The process and the pursuit are the key! Total domination within the mind by positive thoughts will rarely occur. The process and the pursuit are the key!

It is not enough to remove negative thoughts. Removed, negative thoughts must be replaced. If they are not removed and then replaced, negative thoughts will resurface. This crucial point must become a centerpiece of your thinking.

> **It is not enough to remove negative thoughts. Removed, negative thoughts must be replaced. If they are not removed and then replaced, negative thoughts will RESURFACE.**

Accordingly, it is extremely important that we hold fast to the discipline of thinking about the very thoughts we think. We must not only think "negative"

THE KANGAROO FACTOR

and "positive," we must not only think "dump" and "bank," we must also think "remove" and "replace." We must think "leave the postponement-pouch" and "leap with purpose and passion." We must stop doing one thing; we must start doing another thing. This is a central emphasis of *The Kangaroo Factor*.

Removal of the negative without replacement with the positive will equal the postponement-pouch time and again, dream after dream.

The Bank Is A Good Place

When I state that the positive-thought bank is a good place, I am referring to an environment that will pay dividends on your positive thoughts. I speak of a launching pad for your leaping.

As you think about the thoughts you think, do not only think about throwing your negative thoughts in the dump. Ponder taking your positive thoughts to the bank. As you target your thoughts, think about placing your positive thoughts in a very visible bank, somewhere you can see your thoughts anytime you want to see them. (On other occasions, I have referred to this positive-thought bank as a "trophy-thought-display case.")

Take Your Positive Thoughts To The Bank

Naturally, I am not addressing a literal, physical place (however, I do lift up for you again the wisdom of writing down your positive thoughts so they can continue to serve you). At this point, I am addressing a mental place, a high profile positioning of your good and positive thoughts.

Position your thoughts so they can be readily available to service your journey, to inspire you, to encourage you, to help you build dream-steam. I am referring to a high profile depository of your positive thoughts that will enable you to pursue the discipline of mastery, to "help yourself to success," to discover afresh stellar achievement and dream-realization.

Visualize a locale, a mental place, for your positive thoughts. Pull them close to you; hold them within you. Do it for encouragement's sake, for discipline's sake, for your dream's sake.

Keepers

I remember going fishing with my dad. From boat's belly to bank's side, we would fish, sometimes for a very long time.

Often, it would seem as if we would catch every small fish the lake would have to offer. And, of course, Dad would normally say: "Son, take the hook

THE KANGAROO FACTOR

out of the fish's mouth, and let it go. We'll catch him next year, when he is big and plump."

The day would linger on. Then it would happen. Sometimes it would occur at sunset; other times it would take place early the next morning. We would catch the big one, a whopper. And Dad would say, "Now, Son, that is a keeper." Often the "keepers" would mount up. We would head home with a "mess full of keepers."

On one occasion, Dad caught a whale of a "keeper." Why, it was so big that it even made *The Toccoa Record* newspaper. And we had that huge hunk of a fish, that whopper of a "keeper," mounted. I would see that "trophy fish" day after day. Every time I saw it, it brought memories of that fun day, the day Dad and I caught "the keeper."

The great, positive thoughts you have are "keeper" thoughts. They are trophy thoughts. They are hang-on-the-wall thoughts. These great, positive thoughts are take-to-the-bank thoughts.

The displaying of your positive thoughts, the hanging-on-the-wall of your "keepers," the taking of your "keepers" to the bank so that they can pay dividends of growth and achievement, is a smart thing for you to do. Deposit your positive, "keeper-thoughts" in a safe, secure, and dividend-paying place.

Take Your Positive Thoughts To The Bank

> The taking of your "keeper-thoughts" to the bank, so these thoughts can pay dividends of growth and achievement, is the SMART thing for you to do.

"Keeper-thoughts" may resemble:

- "Now, I did handle that well."
- "This is coming along nicely."
- "I expected detours. This is just one of them. I will make it!"

Think about the positive thoughts you think. Take them to the "keeper-bank." Let them grow. Allow them to help you, to nurture your dream-journey. It is not enough to dream big; you must think big. And when you think big thoughts, you must keep them around so they can continue to help you take big steps.

Finders

As a child, I would discover, or find, something very special in the huge fields that bordered my

THE KANGAROO FACTOR

home. Many times, I would be accompanied by friends who would attempt to persuade me that they should have, hold, and keep that which I had found. Whether it was a marble, an old railroad pin, a dollar, or even a Hank Aaron rookie card, I would respond, "Finders, keepers." On rare occasions, I would add, "Losers, weepers."

It is this "Finders, keepers" part that I choose to address here. At this point, however, I choose to address it in reverse order. Here, I refer to "Keepers, finders!" For when you have beneficial thoughts about yourself and your dream, when you hold those thoughts, when you value them as "keepers," there can be some very significant "finders" for you.

You will *find* that:

- "Keeper-thoughts" encourage.
- "Keeper-thoughts" last a long time, if you consistently nurture them.
- "Keeper-thoughts" have a way of spawning, or creating, other positive thoughts.
- "Keeper-thoughts" are contagious and can ooze out to others and encourage them.

Take Your Positive Thoughts To The Bank

A Super Example

I understand that prior to Super Bowl XXXIII in Miami, the exceptional Coach Mike Shanahan of the Denver Broncos did something very wise. He made it possible for the team to "see afresh" on videotape the post-victory celebration of the prior year's victory in Super Bowl XXXII. He and his team found that the viewing of that "keeper" tape was instrumental in encouraging the team to remember the excitement of the year before. They would indeed remember, and they would indeed repeat!

One major "finder" that follows the "keepers" is this – the remembering can cause a remarkable growth, a remarkable discipline, and a remarkable giving in to joy. Keep this thought within your head and heart; allow it to work for you: "When you take your positive thoughts to the bank, when you deposit them in a visible place, when you allow them to grow and to pay dividends, they will work for you."

You will FIND that the REMEMBERING can cause a remarkable growth, a remarkable discipline, and a remarkable giving in to joy.

THE KANGAROO FACTOR

You Can Take It To The Bank

As I was growing up, a certain team would always play another team. Everybody always knew who would win. There was no doubt about it. You could "take it to the bank."

This particular chapter of *The Kangaroo Factor* is being written in early February. It is miserably cold. However, in just three short weeks, our hills of Northeast Georgia will be speckled with daffodils most yellow. There is no doubt about it. Decades have already cast the die. Daffodils will soon trumpet their presence. You can take it to the bank.

Aggravate, pester, and taunt a kangaroo until it becomes very frustrated with you. Drive it to the point of retaliation. It will lean back on its tough tail, box you with its fore limbs, even kick you with its rear feet. You can count on it!

Study, study, study; good grades will follow. Plant and plant, water and water, fertilize and fertilize, and let the sun shine in and shine in again; good crops will follow.

Think about the positive thoughts you think. If you bank them, they can work for you. If you allow them to replace the negative thoughts you have

Take Your Positive Thoughts To The Bank

removed and dumped, then these positive thoughts will help you grow closer to mastering your dream and closer to releasing your best. Count on it. You can take it to the bank! This is a matter of hope – not of hesitation.

More Super Examples

The number of people who have *kept* their positive thoughts and *found* them powerful is legion. Sometimes the keeping was necessary to bring about a second major victory. Other times the keeping of positive thoughts was necessary to bring about a first victory, or even a major comeback. Whatever the circumstances, the "keeping of positive thoughts" can prove to be a vital activity.

Often, the "I can make it" voice will prove to be much weaker than the "you will never make it" voice that others blatantly speak. In the case of you and your dream, this need not prove to be the reality. It certainly was not reality in the lives of these super dreamers who follow. You can find inspiration from a huge and diverse cast of people who were basically told, in one fashion or another, at one time or another, "You will never make it." In varying degrees, others

THE KANGAROO FACTOR

sought to discourage them. Let these persistent dreamers inspire you:

Lance Armstrong	Naomi Judd
Arthur Ashe	Helen Keller
Fred Astaire	Abraham Lincoln
Mudsy Buggs	Billy Payne
Sean Connery	Elvis Presley
Babe Didrikson	Rudy Ruddiger
Walt Disney	Eleanora Sears
Amelia Earhart	Beverly Sills
Thomas Edison	Mother Teresa
Albert Einstein	Sophie Tucker
Doug Flutie	Ted Turner
Clark Gable	Barbara Walters
John Glenn	Spud Webb
Barbara Jordan	The Wright Brothers
Michael Jordan	Oprah Winfrey

Look What They Found

In spite of the circumstances, these persons kept positive thoughts. They held on to their thoughts that were positive in nature. What did they find?

Take Your Positive Thoughts To The Bank

They found massive power in the keeping. They found energy strong enough to propel them out of the "postponement-pouch." By keeping these positive thoughts, by allowing them to circulate within their very being, they became dream conquerors.

Yes, dreamer, you will *find* that there is power in the keeping. There is inertia in the banking of your positive thoughts for purposes of a repeat-victory, a grand slam, or a sweep. There is also potency in the keeping when the issue is the first victory, incremental successes in spite of major detours, or even the supremacy of your inner voice over their "put down" or "put-it-off voice."

There is a place for your positive thoughts. It is the thought-bank. Keep your positive thoughts there. Let them grow dividends for you.

You Are In For A Treat

"You are lucky today," the bell captain said. "You get the finest taxi cab driver on the island, Mr. Tucker. You are really in for a treat!"

The bell captain was correct. Bermuda never seemed so beautiful. It had much to do with Mr. Tucker's commentary. Occasionally, the commentary would be enhanced by Mr. Tucker's philosophy

THE KANGAROO FACTOR

that he most willingly shared. I remember two "nuggets" with which he treated my wife and me.

Let Good Things Circulate In The Mind

At age 72, Mr. Tucker was preparing to leave Bermuda, travel to the University of Florida, and earn a degree in music. He was to leave in a week or two. Mr. Tucker was an accomplished musician who wanted to enhance his skills by further study in music theory. "It is helpful," he stated, "to let good things circulate in the mind."

Mr. Tucker had given us a gift. As you pursue your dream, let good things circulate in your mind. Let grand ideas enter in; allow for no easy escape or early evaporation. Fuel the inner flow. Become the beneficiary of positive ideas. Let them do their work within your inner life cupboard. Enjoy them. Benefit from them. Celebrate the circulation of good things within your mind.

Travel: A Great Form Of Education

Mr. Tucker also indicated that upon completion of his five years of study in Gainesville, Florida,

Take Your Positive Thoughts To The Bank

he and his wife planned to move to New Orleans and then travel. "You know," he said, "one of the finest forms of education is travel."

Travel can birth positive thoughts. Travel can help you retain positive thoughts. Travel *is* educational. It teaches, inspires, and ignites. By traveling, you can build a huge inventory of ideas and inspirations. Travel can become a forum in which good ideas start circulating within your mind.

You can certainly birth your dream at home. The process can also occur in the mountains, near the beach, on an island, by waterfalls, in a meadow, on a cruise ship, overseas, next door, beside a quiet brook, at a ball park, at an amusement park, at a zoo, at a library, in a church, in a garden, on an airplane, and at a museum.

Travel! Let good things circulate within your mind. You and your dream will be in for a treat when you allow good ideas to lodge and circulate within your mind!

Part Four

Seize Your Moments

CHAPTER 11

Empty Or Full?

I was in Syracuse, New York. There was significant time between my presentations to allow for street-strolling. On two occasions, I passed the same empty building. On the last of the two occasions, I stopped and stared into the building. It was huge and dark.

As I started to leave, a white poster board leaning against one of the two huge windowpanes caught my attention. It had obviously been placed there by a real estate company. The sign was simple; there were no graphics, no colors. It featured plain,

THE KANGAROO FACTOR

black lettering. However, in spite of its plain make-up, I will never forget how it read: "This building is not empty. It is full of opportunity."

That sign emphatically told me that what I had seen (a huge, dark, empty building) was, in a very real sense, an illusion. That building was not empty; it was loaded with opportunity. Quite simply, the sign indicated positive thinking, purposeful thinking, and profitable thinking.

You should be inclined to perceive the moments ahead of you as moments full of opportunity. By now you should feel much more comfortable about choosing your city. You should be strongly inclined to select Do City over Could City. You should be much more ready for dream-naming, for dream-awakening, for a giving in to joy. You should be thinking about the very thoughts you think, about throwing your negative thoughts in the dump, about taking your positive thoughts to the bank.

You should be ready to tackle the building – not the building that is empty, but the building that is full of opportunities. By now, you should feel like leaping – not for joy, but with joy! And the exciting thing is this: you have at your disposal the launching pad you will need for seizing your opportunity-moments.

Empty Or Full?

> **By now you should feel like LEAPING –
> not for joy, but with joy!**

A Life-System

Let me remind you that *The Kangaroo Factor* is a system. It is a dreaming and thinking system. It is a life-system. It is a discipline based on big, positive attitude. It is an approach structured around big, positive behavior. It equals the whole that will unfold from this moment on. As you experience *The Kangaroo Factor – Dream Big! Think Big! Seize The Moment!*, hold on to it. Study it. Write in the margins. Underline and highlight. Apply what is appropriate. Allow it to help you leap!

You need not look upon your dream-building as that which is empty. You, and your dream, will be served when you look upon your dream-building as full of opportunities.

When you view your dream-building as full of opportunities, you embody a very powerful thinking-system. You release a life-system that, in reality, equals three in number:

THE KANGAROO FACTOR

- Positive Thinking
- Purposeful Thinking
- Profitable Thinking

Positive Thinking

You read the very sub-heading positioned above this sentence and, in all probability, you think, without hesitation, of Dr. Norman Vincent Peale. If, by chance, you are not familiar with the work of Dr. Peale, I encourage you to refer to the Recommended Reading List that begins on page 267. Through written and spoken word, through act piled upon act, Dr. Peale embodied the "this building is full of opportunities" thinking. (I specifically lift up two works by Dr. Peale: *The Power Of Positive Thinking* and *Imagining.*)

To seize the dream-moments, to go at it full-throttle, is to pull out all the stops. To act upon big dreams, to act upon big thoughts, is to refuse to see the big moments of your life as empty. It is to see your dream-building as full of opportunity. It is to focus not on emptiness, but on potential. It is to focus not on negativity, but on "positiveness." It is to focus not on the postponement-pouch, but on the leaping. It is to focus not on the tiny, timid steps, but on a

Empty Or Full?

dream realization made possible by a bold, systemic, and systematic "big-footedness."

To see full, not empty, even when it might appear as empty to others, is to experience positive, give-in-to-joy thinking as:

- Highly possible ("I can do this.")
- Perception-based ("I already perceive or visualize this happening.")
- Extremely beneficial ("This journey of joy is serving me well.")
- Authentically encouraging ("My dream is not a fantasy. Something real is in the air.")

To see FULL, not empty, even when it might appear as empty to others, is to experience positive, give-in-to-joy thinking!

Your dream-building is full of possibilities, not emptiness. Do you now see those opportunities? They are based on an abundance of realities, including the following:

THE KANGAROO FACTOR

- You do not have to stay the way you are.
- You can do more than you might have ever imagined.
- Your "I can do it" voice will often prove superior to their "You will never do it" voice.
- You do not grow when you find something outside you and then try to place it within you.
- You will grow and soar when you recognize and release what is already within you!
- There is a powerhouse arsenal within you that may have been dormant for decades.

Purposeful Thinking

The last two listings in the previous section were placed there by intent – not by accident. For sake of emphasis and clarity, let me now restate them:

- You will grow and soar when you recognize and release what is already within you!
- There is a powerhouse arsenal within you that may have been dormant for decades.

These two statements serve as a very helpful introduction into "purposeful thinking." I have seen it all across the globe. I have noticed people reaching

Empty Or Full?

outside to find that which is already within them. I have seen persons operating as if excitement, enthusiasm, and even purpose can be somehow absorbed externally. They think they can go out and find this powerful force and then seek to put it within them.

**You will grow and soar when you recognize and release what is already WITHIN you.
There is a powerhouse arsenal within you that may have been DORMANT for decades.**

It Does Not Work Like That

Our best stuff is not out there. It is within us. Unfortunately, many of us spend a lifetime looking for dream-power and dream-purpose out there. We spend a lifetime looking for excitement, satisfaction, and fulfillment out there!

What we must grasp is this: "The core attitudes, the core abilities, the core dreams are already within us." As a matter of fact, they have been within us, perhaps dormant, for decades. For sure, on occasion we will need to acquire new knowledge and learn and apply new skills. For certain, we will need

THE KANGAROO FACTOR

to stay connected to The One named "The Holy Other" by Karl Barth. However, we must do a better job of caring for our "givenness." Our "givenness" needs to be recognized, then refined, then released.

There is much within you now: core attitudes, core abilities, and a core dream. All of this equals your "givenness." All of this is shouting at you, "Let us out. We want to help you grow and soar."

You begin with positive thinking: "I am, I can, I will!" You follow with a pursuit of purpose: "From within, here I go!"

The crucial "seize the life moment" concept that we address here begins with positive thinking and hinges on the pursuit of purposeful thinking. Purpose is never initially found "out there." It is found within you. The necessary attitudes and abilities are not fundamentally found "out there." They are found within you.

It Is Not An Alien Thing

Worded another way, your highest dream-purpose is not an "alien". It is actually an extension of you. Ultimately, you do not find purpose. Purpose finds you. And purpose finds you so very easily because it is already there within you. The same is

Empty Or Full?

true when it comes to appropriate attitudes and appropriate abilities. Ultimately, you do not find them. They find you. And they can do so easily because they are already there within you. (Again, however, your "given" must be enhanced by the "gathered" if you are to experience ultimate growth.)

There is purpose within you that wants to be set loose. There are appropriate attitudes and abilities within you that want to be set loose. Do it!

The Blockage-Problem

But there is a problem. There is blockage. The releasing is much more difficult because of the blockage. Something is standing in the way of the dream-purpose. Something is blocking appropriate attitudes, appropriate abilities, and productive behavior!

The many names we have given to the blockage include:

- Could City
- Dream Block
- Torture Tool
- Fear Fabricator
- Comparison Creator

THE KANGAROO FACTOR

- Horrible Composite
- Postponement-Pouch
- Timid, Tiny Steps

At this point, I want to give another name to the blockage: "Camouflage." For our purposes, camouflage is a myriad of confusion that blends its "obviousness" into a backdrop of external "phonies."

Worded another way, camouflage equals a move to get us thinking that the dream-purpose and dream-power is out there, not within us. It seeks to camouflage the real thing with a concoction of confusion. This confusion is as superficial and as phony as a storefront mannequin. We must be very careful lest CONFUSION clouds CLARITY.

CAMOUFLAGE equals a move to get us thinking that the dream-purpose and dream-power is out there, not within us.

Remove The Camouflage

We must remove the camouflage and call a dream a "dream." Then call it forth, "from within."

Empty Or Full?

Then become immersed in its very purposefulness. We must remove anything that denies us purpose, or reason, or necessity, or calling, or challenge, or dream, or joy!

Camouflage keeps you from seeing the purpose within you, the positive attitudes within you, the phenomenal abilities within you, the "dream big" capacity within you, the "think big" capacity within you, the "seize the moment" capacity within you! Camouflage can goof you up. To see more clearly, you must remove the camouflage that causes you to focus out there instead of within yourself. For sure, the people and the information out there can help you. But first and foremost you must look within.

Look Within

Do not look out there. Look within. That is where you and your purpose will find each other. Purposeful thinking equals a perpetual glance within, a glance within that will provide you with grounding, guidance, growth, and gratitude.

An interesting observation must be addressed at this point. Many of us blame people and events "out there" for our problems. We rationalize that we could be dreaming larger dreams, thinking larger

THE KANGAROO FACTOR

thoughts, seizing our moments more effectively, if other people and events "out there" did not cause us so many problems. However, we also act, from time to time, as if these same people, these same events, have and hold all the answers for us. We act as if they hold the capacity to solve our dream-riddle, have the ability to answer our dream-questions, possess the key to unlock any "caughtness" in which we find ourselves.

Some of the time we look out there and we say: "There, that's where you'll find my problem. It is them, the bad guys and the bad events." Other times we say: "There, that's where the answers to my problem are. The answers equal the good guys and the good events."

If you have to remove some camouflage before you can see clearly the purpose-thinking that is within you, then remove it. Perhaps it will help you to remember that this removal of the camouflage can be a springboard, a perpetual launching pad for the leaping. Removal of camouflage can enable you to see and appreciate that which is within you, your dream-purpose. Your dream-purpose is important enough to be named Compass, or True North, or Anchor, or Rudder. Purpose-thinking provides you with the whole package.

Empty Or Full?

> The REMOVAL of the camouflage can be a springboard, a perpetual launching pad for the leaping.

The Total Dream-Package

Remove the camouflage. You will see more clearly. Look within yourself. You will see your dream-purpose. And when you see and think dream-purpose, you will discover The Total Package. You will discover Compass. You will discover True North. You will discover Anchor. You will discover Rudder. You will feel as if your dream-building, already full with opportunities, is now literally overflowing.

Let me be bold enough to state that the Total Dream-Package is so rooted in purpose as to ultimately die without purpose. Dream-purpose thinking is crucial to your growth. Your dream will remain pouch-bound without purpose.

On The Wings Of Purpose

Allow your purpose to grab you, to flow within your very being, to mesmerize you. Become

THE KANGAROO FACTOR

enticed and excited by your purpose-call. Channel your excitement-based thoughts into your achievement-system. Then strategize – and strategize more!

Bless your strategy with your God-given skills. Sculpt and redefine. Polish those skills. Enhance your skills with the skills and insights of others. Read. Listen. Observe. Blend your system, your strategy, your skills, your enhancement from the skills of others. Keep blending until you succeed. Then soar. Soar on the wings of purpose, purpose from within you!

> **The STRATEGY plus the SKILLS equals the SOARING.**

Remember: Your soaring erupts from within, from your very being. It releases itself from within before it reveals itself from without, in your very doing. Ultimately, you can never do your best purpose-thinking, your best purpose-preparation, your best purpose-pursuit, your best purpose-unleashing, until you first remove your camouflage-based blockage. Remove it. Then look within yourself. You will find that "within" is your dream-purpose's best starting-place!

Empty Or Full?

Your thinking positively positions you to look within and to respond purposefully! Your thinking purposefully will pay big dividends, both in your dream-leaping and in your dream-landing.

Profitable Thinking

Your dream-building is not only full of positive opportunities and purposeful opportunities; it is also full of profitable opportunities. Remember, a chief concept addressed throughout *The Kangaroo Factor* in general, and in this chapter in particular, is that profit shows its face in two settings:

- Critical-response moments (rare and special)
- Life-system moments (special during the whole of your life)

A Perpetual Surprise

To be involved in profitable thinking is to be perpetually surprised by a powerhouse statement: "Benefit does not equal a curse; benefit equals a blessing."

This does come as a surprise to many of us because we are more experienced with sacrifice than benefit, more experienced with struggle than success and soaring. We are more experienced with denial than acceptance, even more experienced with giving than receiving.

From time to time, I tell myself something like this: "It is all right for me to think thoughts that will benefit me and others. I was not created to stumble and struggle forever. I was created to soar. And when I do soar, To Him Be The Glory."

Inoculate yourself against the thinking that carries with it the thought that life must always equal incessant burden. Become the beneficiary of this perpetual surprise: "You can experience joy, fulfillment, and meaningful profit in your thinking and in your dreaming."

Just Around The Corner?

Something very exciting may soon occur within your dream-building. Your most exciting moments may be yet-to-be and close-at-hand. Right now, you may hold within your head and heart a powerhouse of an idea. Let me state this to you most emphatically: "A positive, purposeful, and profitable idea is a 'soaring' waiting to happen." Something good may be just around the corner for you.

Empty Or Full?

> A positive, purposeful, and profitable idea is a SOARING waiting to happen.

Think on the positive side. Visualize that dream-building as one that is full of possibilities. Stop living in the land of "never, never; not me, not me." Visit a more exciting land – not a barren land, but a bountiful land, a land full of dream-opportunities for you. And, when you enter this land, seize its opportunities!

If You Talk Up A Storm, Make It A Spring Shower

Another will ask, "Who is that talking up a storm?" I am normally the culprit. I do like to talk. That is a fact.

Now, the phrase "talking up a storm" has a significance for us because that is precisely what many of us do in relationship to our dreams. When it comes to seizing the very opportunity-moments of our dream, we "talk up a storm." Sometimes that is good; other times that is bad.

THE KANGAROO FACTOR

For our purposes, "talking up a storm" equals one of three different things:

- Smoke and fire (talk and waste)
- Blowing smoke (all talk, no walk)
- Spring showers (the bursting out of the new)

Smoke And Fire

This type of storm is, of course, destructive in nature. It is based on negativity. It does your dreaming no good. It discourages big thoughts and big actions. Its lightning equals a damaging, anti-self talk. There is thick confusion, intense apprehension, the burning away of resources. Negative, "smoke and fire" talk attacks the very energy behind your dream.

Blowing Smoke

This is procrastinating in nature. It is based in perpetual postponement, perhaps even hypocrisy. Its activity equals a smoldering "big-talker" mentality. It becomes a smoldering that never equals a visual and verifiable dream-ignition.

Empty Or Full?

Spring Showers

This is positive and highly beneficial in nature. It is based on wise choices, named and awakened dreams, positive thoughts, and "making the best of each situation." Its occurrences produce new growth. Exciting things will pop up all over the place. Its growth-system equals the persistent and steady rains of positive thinking, purposeful thinking, and profitable thinking.

The Seizer's Vocabulary

One who knows when to seize rare and fleeting moments, and steady dream-life moments as well, must understand how important it is to monitor self-talk.

The storm you "talk up" must not equal "smoke and fire." Neither must it equal "nothing but smoke." The storm you "talk up" must equal "spring showers." The spring showers will equal big dreams, big thoughts, seized moments, giving in to joy!

Your self-talk defines your dream. It defines the direction of your subsequent thoughts. It defines the discipline of your approach. Your self-talk determines whether you experience the discipline of misery

THE KANGAROO FACTOR

(helpless, hurting) or the discipline of mastery (hopeful, helpful). What you say to yourself about yourself can equal aggravating frustration or awesome fulfillment. It can equal the "empty." Or it can equal the "full."

> **Your self-talk determines whether you experience the discipline of MISERY (helpless, hurting) or the discipline of MASTERY (hopeful, helpful).**

I thought it might be helpful to categorically list what I call negative self-talk ("smoke and fire" and "nothing but blowing smoke") and positive self-talk ("spring showers") trigger words. I do this to underscore the importance of our self-talk, fully understanding that some of the issues raised by these very words have already been addressed. Any repetition will serve a necessary function of restatement.

Negative Self-Talk

- I do not stand a chance.
- I am unworthy.
- I cannot do it now.

Empty Or Full?

- This is not me.
- I will embarrass myself.
- I will be ridiculed.
- No matter how hard I try, it will not work.
- It's just not possible.
- I dwell on the "empty" side.
- I will make a fool of myself.
- I will get around to it one day.
- I just have more than I can handle.
- I cannot fit it in.
- I cannot measure up.
- I cannot leap.
- I do not know.
- I just "do not understand."
- I will be miserable.

Positive Self-Talk

- Yes, it will work.
- In the face of adversity, I can prevail.
- Nothing will stand in my way.
- It is up to me.
- I already see it happening.
- Yes, this is my moment.
- I have done it before; I will do it again.
- I dwell on the "full" side.

THE KANGAROO FACTOR

- I will do "the big" in little chunks.
- This is my responsibility.
- I will celebrate incremental finishedness.
- I will reward myself.
- One moment will change my life.
- I can be the beneficiary of change.
- Success is only a comeback away.
- I can build dream-steam.
- I can leap; and I can land!
- I will experience mastery.

There Is Logic In The List

Study this vocabulary. Add your own words and phrases to it. Keep it highly visible. This may prove to be refrigerator-front stuff, under-the-desktop stuff, front-of-daily-calendar stuff. Use it. Seize it time and again. Let it help you when appropriate.

Let it help you choose your city. Enable it to lead you to Do City. Permit it to bless your named dream, your awakened dream. Give in to its joy-assistance. Allow it to service your thought-life. Authorize it to help you throw your negative thoughts in the dump. Give it permission to help you take your positive thoughts to the bank. Grant it the privilege

Empty Or Full?

to serve your positive thinking, your purposeful thinking, and your profitable thinking.

There is logic in the list. Ponder it. It will help you figure out, or reason out, how your self-talk is affecting the realization of your dream.

Seize this list and the very concepts it represents. Take this to the bank: "Your negative self-talk will discourage you and your dream; your positive self-talk will encourage you and your dream."

As you study this list, as you add to it and personalize it, you will be encouraged to delete "empty" from your vocabulary. You will be encouraged to highlight "full" and "opportunities" and "mastery" in your vocabulary.

CHAPTER 12

Mystery, Misery, Or Mastery?

I barely made it. However, after my final six weeks at ROTC Camp at Fort Bragg, North Carolina, I was commissioned an officer in the United States Army. Shortly after I learned that I had made it, I asked the commanding officer, "Why?" He responded in somewhat of a whimsical fashion, "I do not know, Stephen. It is a mystery to me. I do know, however, that it was not by consensus."

That was not the only time I heard the word "mystery" during that six week period. Almost every

THE KANGAROO FACTOR

other day, during mess, we would be served the standard rice, potatoes, or greens. Whatever had blessed our plate would often be cursed with a chunk of something indescribable. Upon inquiry, my comrades and I would learn that the slab was meat. No one would ever tell us precisely what type of meat was on our plate. Accordingly, we unanimously agreed to name the meat we reluctantly received as "mystery meat."

Mystery

We named the meat "mystery meat" because we did not know what it was. Certainly, you might not know, detail by detail, what your dream-future holds for you. But you should have an idea. There should be little mystery about it. By now you should certainly know that your dream should be grounded in joy, that it should have a definite name, a purpose, and that it awaits your wake-up call.

For each of us, there should come a time when we do know what our dream is. There should come a time when we should be willing to act in response to our dream. There should come a time when we delete the early Aborigines' definition of "kangaroo" – "I do not know; I do not understand" – from our vocabulary. Perpetual postponement clouds the issue.

Mystery, Misery, Or Mastery?

> PERPETUAL POSTPONEMENT will cloud your thinking if you repeatedly remain uncertain about the specifics of your dream.

Any crucible or habitat that is without a dream-plan becomes a breeding place for uncertainty. Here, uncertainty equals a huge mystery, a mystery totally void of joy. It becomes a mystery that is so powerful that it destroys enthusiasm. It equals a mystery that is so powerful that it diminishes direction, discipline, and delight. It becomes a mystery so superior that it wipes out fun and fulfillment.

Something must replace the mystery. Replacement must occur soon. A "no-idea-which-way-to-go" mentality is very dangerous. Mystery can certainly lead to something worse. It can lead to misery. Suspense can lead to significant struggle.

> A "NO-IDEA-WHICH-WAY-TO-GO" mentality is very dangerous. Mystery can certainly lead to something worse. It can lead to misery!

THE KANGAROO FACTOR

Misery

When one allows joy-mystery, purpose-mystery, and plan-mystery to escalate, confusion becomes very powerful. When one repeatedly allows confusion to dominate over clarity, chaos can be the result.

Mystery left unattended, mystery that runs wild, can equal misery for you.

It hurts me to say this, because in many situations it will not be true. However, I must say it – "Sometimes it can be too late." There are indeed moments that should be seized now, not later.

For sure, our very existence must be perpetually informed and influenced by the Gospel of the Second Chance as it relates to our spirit. However, if mystery clouds the "now" too much and too long, the end result may be missed opportunity, remorse, joylessness, and misery!

As painful as it is for me to write this, let me do it now: "Your dream-building that is now full of joy-opportunities may not always be as full of the same opportunities." As much as I believe success may only be a comeback away, I must write that prolonged dream-mystery can eventually bring on misery.

Mystery, Misery, Or Mastery?

However, there is another option. You do not have to relate to your moments as if they are nothing but mystery. You have another choice than to repeatedly hold hands with misery. Your third option, far more powerful than mystery (uncertainty) or misery (chaos) is mastery (a system most superior).

Mastery

It is not enough to choose Do City over Could City. It will not suffice to merely name a dream, awaken that dream, and give in to joy. To target your thoughts, to think about the very thoughts you think, to throw your negative thoughts to the dump, and to take your positive thoughts to the bank is not enough.

You must grab with all of your being the very adhesive that binds choosing to dreaming and thinking to seizing. This bonding agent, this adhesive, equals a system. The system actually must become a regimen. The regimen must become a discipline! There is no room for timidity.

Since your doing actually emerges out from your being, since you already have within you what you need, you choose to discipline yourself in order to reach your dream-joy.

THE KANGAROO FACTOR

No discipline may be more effective than self-discipline. No discipline may be more difficult than self-discipline. Effectiveness and difficulty often travel together.

> **No discipline may be more EFFECTIVE than self-discipline. No discipline may be more DIFFICULT than self-discipline.**

If discipline initially fails to work for you, you must refuse to push the shift-the-blame button. You must simply choose to master your self-discipline, to "systematically and systemically," "regularly and rigorously," order your attitudes and behavior. Rarely is this an easy task! Never will someone else be able to do it for you!

To master your self-discipline is to reach your highest bar and then raise it. It may appear as ironic at first, but the mastering of your self-discipline and the practice of the discipline of mastery travel hand in hand. Both are process; neither is event.

Mystery, Misery, Or Mastery?

> To MASTER your self-discipline is to reach your highest bar and then raise it.

The Practice Process

The last two sentences in the preceding paragraph are very important. Please read them afresh. And please understand that there are two key words that I choose to address at this point: "practice" and "process."

Please note that doctors and lawyers are required to study and study, to graduate and graduate, to work and to work. Yet, decades into their work, when asked what they do, they respond accordingly: "I practice medicine." "I practice law."

Inherent in the very discipline related to the study of medicine and law is perpetual practice. Inherent in the very discipline related to your dream-design, your dream-destiny, and your dream-realization, is perpetual practice. Let me be bold enough here to state that dream-joy will never be fully experienced without perpetual practice.

To master self-discipline is to practice the discipline of mastery, the discipline of reaching and then

THE KANGAROO FACTOR

raising the bar. It is to understand that mastery-arrival is always an enigma. Mastery is not only perpetual practice; it is also perpetual process. Ultimately, finishedness does not equal reality; it equals the goal. And ultimately, the goal can always be redefined.

> **Mastery-arrival is always an ENIGMA. It never ends, yet it can always begin again. The practice process never finishes.**

For this very reason, "mastery" rarely retires. From Senator John Glenn to President Jimmy Carter, from King Hussein to Mother Teresa, we have seen instances of mastery celebrated and examples of mastery at work.

The "Reach Advantage"

Just last night, prior to the televised boxing match, the announcer shared with the audience what he referred to as "the tale of the tape." It included descriptive comparisons between the two fighters, broken down into weight, height, and the like. I was

Mystery, Misery, Or Mastery?

particularly intrigued by one comparison, that which was related to reach. The fighter with the longer arm-reach supposedly held what many considered to be the "reach advantage" over the other fighter. Presumably, a longer reach benefited him both offensively and defensively.

As we begin to approach book's end, please allow me to indicate to you, as strongly as I know how, that to give in to joy, to dream big, to think big, and to seize the moment, you must have the "reach advantage." You will never hold that "reach advantage" until you first learn to perpetually practice the discipline of dream-joy mastery!

How To Do It

The answer is in the system. Now is the time for you to move beyond the frustrating symptoms of dream-joylessness. Now is the time for you to throw the frustrating symptoms of mystery and misery where they belong; throw them in the dump!

Now is the time for you to move beyond the *symptom-based* frustration that has ruined your days and nights. Move to the *system-based* fulfillment that can cause you to go to bed at night satisfied about your dream-progress. Move to the system that can lead to mastery.

Specifically, now is the time for you to:

- Be professional.
- Be process-focused.
- Be plan-centered.
- Be preparation-grounded.
- Be prophetic.
- Be positive.
- Be personal.

Be Professional

Profess. Shout. Exclaim. Unleash your highest and best attitudes and behavior. Whatever your dream-base (sales, education, leadership, networking, ministry, law, engineering, medicine, business), be professional.

Be sure that there is consistency or integrity within you. Your whole being must relate to itself in a consistent, not hypocritical, fashion. Let all that is within you correspond with itself in such a professional way as to convince you that you are a person of integrity. Look like you sound.

Mystery, Misery, Or Mastery?

Be professional about your dream. Profess it with head and heart. Be professional from the very start (the leaping). And you will be enabled to be professional at the various endings (landings).

> **Let all that is within you correspond with itself in such a professional way as to convince you that you are a person of INTEGRITY.**

Be Process-Focused

When you are frustrated, stay away from elevators: "In case of fire, do not take the elevators, take the steps." Seek to understand that the unleashing of one's personal self, the unfolding of one's professionalism, does not occur as an elevator-event. It reveals itself in process, step by step.

Understand afresh that giving into dream-joy is not always easy. Often, you must become the beneficiary of time, expert advice, support-help, even traveling by detour. However, when you accept and focus on the process, rather than perpetually wish for the event, you can discover dream-joy during both the journey and the destination.

THE KANGAROO FACTOR

Be Plan-Centered

Never "wish it" to happen. "Plan it" to happen. Unfortunately, many of us grew up hearing much more about "planets" (Jupiter, Saturn, and the like) than we did "plan-its."

Whereas a "planet" may be something far away that is very intriguing, our "plan-its" are very close at hand and very important. When your dream-joy is plan-centered, when you have a well-defined "plan-it," you have something that is meaningful, monitorable, and measurable. You have something that can be mastered!

> Your "PLAN-IT" should be specific, monitorable, measurable, and close at hand.

Be Preparation-Grounded

Throw "winging it" and "finessing your way through" in the dump. Remember: "Prepared places are for prepared people." Remember: "Avoidance is rarely as powerful as actualization." Remember:

Mystery, Misery, Or Mastery?

"Postponement or procrastination is rarely as powerful as realization."

Joy rarely flies on wings named anything other than "Preparation." Ground your joy in significant, sweaty, solid preparation.

> **Joy rarely flies on wings named anything other than "PREPARATION."**

Be Prophetic

When pondering your dream name and wake-up call, visualize need. Visualize need seized. Visualize opportunity. Visualize opportunity seized. Visualize accomplishment. Visualize accomplishment seized.

In your head and in your heart, visualize what the results will look like. Be leery of thought-evaporation here. Put those thoughts in writing. Keep them visible. Read them often. The thought plus the writing equals the launching pad for moments seized and moments mastered. Your writing-it-down can be a first step in giving life to your prophetic-side.

THE KANGAROO FACTOR

> **Be leery of THOUGHT EVAPORATION. Put your visualized dream-joy thoughts in writing.**

Be Positive

"Positiveness" pays off. It opens doors. It swings them wide. It places a hook into a hole at the door's top, keeping the door wide open.

"Positiveness" works. It leads to dream-moments seized, to dream-moments mastered, and to dream-moments celebrated.

You will never be *positive* about your dream as long as you refuse to be *personal* about your dream. Personalize your dream, lest it fade into the land of the boring and the bland.

> **You will never be POSITIVE about your dream as long as you refuse to be PERSONAL about your dream.**

Mystery, Misery, Or Mastery?

Be Personal

Know yourself. Understand yourself. Be yourself.

In many ways, we have saved the most significant of our mandated challenges (be professional, be process-focused, be plan-centered, be process-grounded, be prophetic, be positive, and be personal) for last. I did this for a reason. What you will read in these next few paragraphs will dramatically inform and influence the previous mandates.

When I write "be personal," I challenge you. I challenge you to:

- Sing your song.
- Loosen your limits.
- Sculpt your strengths.

Sing Your Song

Sing your song. Dance your dance. Honor your heart. Do not die without having lived. Celebrate your "just-oneness."

About a week ago, I was at a funeral, paying my respects to a precious family. I saw many people that I had not seen for decades. One lady approached

THE KANGAROO FACTOR

me and asked that dreadful question, "Do you recognize me?" In this instance, I responded, "No." She told me that she had heard me on the radio earlier that week. She then proceeded to tell me that we had not seen each other in thirty-five years. I would learn that she was one of my classmates in Mrs. Vaughan's typing class back in 1964.

Then she said something very nice, "I sat behind you and watched the way you were. You sat up front and were always doing things differently. I knew then that you would find your place and make a difference."

I was taken back, in part because of the time and the place. I thanked her for what she said. But I did not say what I should have said. I hope I will get another chance. I should have said, "Jane, we all have a place. I am sure you make a difference as well. I am just loud and out front. The real special ones are the ones that remember way back when, and then remember to encourage."

We are all special. One by one, we do have a song to sing, a dance to dance, a heart to honor. Personalize your dream. Make your difference. Sew your seed. Drive your engine.   Leap your leaps.

Mystery, Misery, Or Mastery?

> We are all special. One by one, we do have a SONG to sing, a DANCE to dance, a HEART to honor. Personalize your dream.
> Make your difference.

Loosen Your Limits

The verb here is "loosen," not "lose." Recognize your limits. Separate those limits that can be modified and corrected from those limits about which you can do little. Refuse to be totally constrained by every limit you face. Again, arm yourself with the tool of discernment.

> SEPARATE those limits that can be modified and corrected from those limits about which you can do little.

I love to tell the story about Snickers and Cecil. They are our two cats – our two indoor cats. Accordingly, for the sake of furniture and the like, and for our sake, Snickers and Cecil have been de-clawed.

THE KANGAROO FACTOR

But, do not tell them that. With regularity and precision, and surely some frustration, Snickers and Cecil still attempt to sharpen their claws.

When I write "loosen your limits," I am saying two things:

- There are some limits you should recognize and drop. Then you move on.
- There are other limits you should recognize, modify, and improve. Then you move on.

Examine And Sort Your Limits

There are limits that we need to recognize because they are hurting us. We waste our time when we try to do certain things that we should not be trying to do.

Quite frankly, there are times when we should see the power of our limits. We should stop fueling the internal combustion that leads to little more than spin-wheeling. We should find ourselves a more appropriate dream.

We should be so committed to appropriate, big dreams that we stop trying to sharpen claws we do not have. As an example, one rarely notices the

Mystery, Misery, Or Mastery?

kangaroo swimming, walking, or running. The kangaroo is committed to leaping.

> **We should be so COMMITTED to big dreams, to big thinking, to moments seized and mastered, and to dream joy that we stop trying to sharpen claws we do not have.**

It is not always easy to separate the limits that must be discarded from the limits that we can modify and improve. Sometimes we will need a series of tests or a gathering of second opinions. I know the tests can be wrong. The second opinions can be wrong as well. But they can be right.

You have to choose. You can be fundamentally led by self-analysis, prayer, and this fact: "The recognition of your limits is not bad, it is good." When you find yourself "sharpening claws that you do not have," stop wasting your time; move on. Comprehension and release of this genre of limits can help you grow your appropriate dreams.

There is a second type of limits which should not be discarded, but corrected and modified. Again, our discernment comes into play here. Sometimes,

THE KANGAROO FACTOR

with a tweak here and a tweak there, we can adjust a limit without discarding it.

This Example May Help

At this writing, I have given several thousand presentations. I have learned much about myself. For example, I have discovered that I do not function well when I am hot. And if you have ever seen me speak, you know I get hot in a hurry.

How do I respond? In most situations, I do two things:

- I take off my coat (discard it).
- I loosen my tie (modify it).

I know what to discard. I know what to modify.

As you pursue the discipline of dream-mastery, you will learn more and more from your experiences. As you pursue the discipline of mastery, you will learn more and more about filtering your limits, about separating that which you can discard from that which you can modify.

Recognize your limits. Recognize their impact. Respond by discarding some of your limits, stop dwelling on them. Move on, perhaps toward a

Mystery, Misery, Or Mastery?

new dream if necessary. Respond by modifying some of your limits. Continue working on them. Utilize your gift of discernment. When appropriate, seek help.

As you benefit from your own dream-related experiences and from the sound advice of others, you will eventually learn when to "take off your coat" and when to simply "loosen your tie."

> **As it relates to limits, and how they impact your dream, RECOGNIZE THE DIFFERENCE between discarding and modifying.**

Sculpt Your Strengths

My heart beats a little faster as I write this particular section in Chapter Twelve. For more than a quarter of a century, I have been addressing the sizzle and pizzazz associated with strength affirmation and strength sculpting.

Often, this has unfolded as a challenge for others to recognize their capacity to thrive on confronting the weaknesses of their team members effectively, while at the same time affirming the

THE KANGAROO FACTOR

strengths of their team members so ineptly. I have challenged others to stop being so good at Loss Reviews and to start doing much better at Win Reviews with their team members. I have reminded them that their associates grow most effectively not when they put down their associates (that is when their associates will self-destruct), but when they affirm their associates (that is when their associates will self-correct).

Here, I address you, your dream, and your joy. Encourage yourself at the point of your strengths. Participate in your own Win Reviews. Value your own leaping and landing capacity! This is very appropriate. As a matter of fact, becoming "personal" about your own Win Reviews is highly advantageous toward your dream.

**You do not grow when you incessantly put yourself down. That is when you self-destruct.
You GROW when you affirm yourself
at the point of your strengths.
That is when you SELF-CORRECT.**

Mystery, Misery, Or Mastery?

Underneath – All The Time

I am always losing something – car keys, change, hotel keys. Invariably, I look underneath something else and find what I lost. Stop looking everywhere else for your dream. Your dream-stuff has been underneath your skin, within you, all the time.

An emphasis of our time together, and a major concept to be celebrated afresh at this point, is this: "The stuff of big dreams, big thoughts, moments seized, and moments mastered is not out there. It is underneath your skin, within you."

Strength-sculpting has much to offer you. It also mandates much from you. Strength-sculpting begins with an "inner journey." There are eight pre-requisites to effective strength-sculpting:

- Stop looking without. That can be a "nowhere" land.
- See within. You have the seizing stuff, the attitude, the abilities. They are already there within you.
- Study consistently. Nourish your strength with study. Love to read.

THE KANGAROO FACTOR

- Start applying. Use your strength-muscle. Learn from doing.
- Seize every opportunity. Do not sit around and wait. Jump at the chance.
- Strive to sculpt. Allow discernment, perception, experience, study, second opinions, and intense effort to help you mold your strengths.
- Serve Him. Remember He is the source of every strength.
- Serve others. Allow your strength-sculpting to benefit others.

Recognize Your Connections

Your looking within, your sculpting your strengths, should not deny you the right to recognize and utilize your connections. On the contrary, it should enhance your connections. Be disciplined at this point; comprehend within head and heart the connections you possess, connections that will help you seize your moments of opportunity and mastery. The two, your best self and your connections, need not work against each other; they can work with each other. Together they can benefit your dream.

Mystery, Misery, Or Mastery?

My first book would have never been published had I not recognized and utilized my "connectedness" to others who were willing to help me. In order to maximize my "connectedness," I developed a technique that I now refer to as R-E-N-T-S.

Before I share R-E-N-T-S with you, I want to encourage you to develop and outline your personal model for benefiting from your "connectedness." My plan, a system that has now served me for more than a decade, may not work for you. If my sharing serves as an inspiration or as an idea starter for you, then that may be cause for celebration.

R-E-N-T-S

R-E-N-T-S equaled the utilization of the following to assist me in the accomplishment of my dreams:

- Relatives
- Encouragers
- Neighbors
- Teachers
- Student

THE KANGAROO FACTOR

Before I elaborate on this model, I want to share a caution with you: "Any strength taken too far can prove to be problematical." In some cases, the advice from others in relationship to your dream can prove to be inappropriate and destructive.

Let me be so bold as to state this: "It is possible that fierce and misplaced opposition to you and your dream can surface from those whom you considered to be your closest relatives and your closest friends." This will be addressed later in more detail under a subheading entitled "Dream Hinderers." For now, remember this: "It is possible that the attitude and behavior of another will not necessarily be 'a caring enough to confront.'" It may more closely resemble a deliberate and self-serving sabotaging of your dream. It may be driven by another's self-serving agenda, rather than an agenda for encouraging you.

With that caution stated, let me briefly outline for you how R-E-N-T-S became an instrumental tool in my dream-journey of becoming an author.

Relatives

- My cousin   Attorney (copyright, patent) – a first line enthusiast
- My mother   Genuine supporter – "caring enough to confront"

Mystery, Misery, Or Mastery?

Encouragers

- NSA — A cadre of peers par excellence – a blending of diverse "second opinions" from members of the National Speakers Association

Neighbors

- Next mile — Typesetter – so close by
- Next door — Printer – that extra effort

Teachers

- English — Editor – minimizing the errors

Student

- Speech 101 — Typist – speeding the process

"Particularized"

Please note that my dream-support system was "particularized" or "personalized." My arsenal of dream enthusiasts included: my cousin, my mother, my fellow NSA members, my close-by neighbors, my former teachers, and my former student.

Your nexus of support, your "connectedness" will differ vastly from mine. This is the way it should be. You do not want to "copycat" my system. You do not want to duplicate any other person's system. You should demand that your system be precisely that – **your** system.

Build A System

Avoid dream-misery. Transcend dream-mystery. Experience dream-mastery.

"Gift" yourself with a system – not my R-E-N-T-S system, but your own system. Benefit your dream with a structure that enables you to maximize your connections. Construct a model that enables you to transform symptoms of frustration into systems of dream-fulfillment.

The development of your dream-mastery system will necessitate yet another discernment-step. As you build your mastery-support system, you must discern between "dream hinderers" and "dream helpers."

Mystery, Misery, Or Mastery?

Dream Hinderers

Several years ago, I considered purchasing a business. I sought the advice of others before I totally immersed myself into my dream.

One of the persons with whom I talked was an expert in this particular field of work. Before I purchased the business, I thought it would be appropriate to spend some time with this particular expert.

We met. In both indirect and direct fashion, he dissuaded me from purchasing the business. I followed his advice.

Although I must take complete responsibility for my actions, I must also note that this same person later purchased the business that he advised me not to pursue. In retrospect, I wonder if he brought "purity of motive" into our time together.

For our purposes, there are three types of dream-hinderers:

- Competition
- Family Members
- Cheerleaders

THE KANGAROO FACTOR

Competition

Some will oppose your dream with the fear that it might jeopardize their agenda and their success. (This was perhaps illustrated in the preceding scenario listed under "Dream Hinderers.")

Competition can certainly create a crucible for jealousy, hidden motives, gossip, and dogged resistance.

This is not always the case. There are certainly exceptions to this rule. One phenomenal exception that I refer to so often is the National Speakers Association. It is comprised of almost 4,000 professional speakers, many of whom are vying for the same engagements. However, the members of this association equal the "best of the best" when it comes to authentically sharing with, and helping, each other.

In many instances, however, be leery of your competition when you seek to build your dream. Be aware of this: "Your competition's agenda may repeatedly rise above your dream-agenda."

Family Members

Discouragers often wear costumes that camouflage their spirit. One costume that discouragers often wear is that of "family member."

Mystery, Misery, Or Mastery?

You might automatically expect that your family members would occupy first place in the list that equals your cadre of dream-supporters. This will certainly, on occasion, prove to be the case. However, often this will prove to be very far from the truth.

For reasons that are too complex to address in a single book, family members may not always serve as allies to your dream. Family members, on occasion, may actually serve as your dream-enemy.

I mention this as a mode of warning: "Do not assume that family members will be first in line to support you and your dream."

Family members may eventually equal "dream-hinderers" for reasons of jealousy, incompetency, or lack of objectivity. Again, this will not always prove to be the case. Family members may certainly help bring vigor, virtue, and victory to you and your dream. The lesson here is this: "Exercise caution."

Cheerleaders

On first reading, the subheading "Cheerleaders" may appear as that which is in error. One, if inclined, could argue that cheerleaders stand apart from competitors and family members with hidden

THE KANGAROO FACTOR

agendas. Unfortunately, many so-called "cheerleaders" bring as much potential harm to you and your dream as do ruthless competitors and jealous family members.

There is of course one significant variable to be considered here. Whereas some competitors and some family members will seek to harm your dream by *intent*, some cheerleaders will impede your dream by *accident*.

For sure, some cheerleaders are intentionally violating any modicum of authenticity or integrity. They are simply throwing "good words" your way. In this case, the words are empty.

However, I lift up "cheerleaders" as potential "dream-hinderers", not because of any meanness or lack of integrity, but because of a naivety or lack of objectivity.

Earlier in *The Kangaroo Factor*, I referred to my tendency to elicit help from relatives, encouragers, neighbors, teachers, and students. Whenever I solicited the help of another, I received enthusiastic support. However, in a limited number of cases, the persons who cheered me with a magnificent level of intensity brought with them no discernment, no objectivity, no knowledge about my qualifications, and no valid insight into my dream.

Mystery, Misery, Or Mastery?

I should not have enlisted the help of such a cadre of inappropriate, and eventually ineffective, cheerleaders. When an error in judgment was made here, it was my responsibility. Again, a word of caution is essential. Choose your cheerleaders CAREFULLY.

Simply because someone cheers you and your dream on in a particular circumstance, does not mean you and your dream should be cheered in a particular circumstance. Please, let me encourage you to be certain that any cheerleading in relationship to your dream is based on the value and potential of your dream rather than the exuberance of cheerleaders who bring little more than naivety to task. Be very leery here. Refuse to be misled by a noisy cheerleader who yells encouragement from within a barrel called "naivety."

Mastering The Hinderers

The effective dreamer will isolate those persons who negatively impact his or her dream. In this instance, "isolation" refers to a "setting aside" that enables the dreamer to be less vulnerable to the negative influence of "dream-hinderers."

THE KANGAROO FACTOR

For sake of review, this sifting-process equals:

- Filtering the advice of competitors through the sieve of motive
- Weighing the influence of family members on an agenda-scale
- Monitoring the merit of cheerleaders through a gauge that monitors both objectivity and competency

Dream Helpers

Misery is eliminated, mystery is transcended, and mastery is celebrated when you encounter the grace and the courage to receive assistance from dream helpers. Your very capacity to receive help from others can have great impact on the realization of your dream.

You will be one significant step closer to dream mastery when you learn to categorize your dream helpers as:

- Those who talk
- Those who listen
- Those who confront
- Those who have written

Mystery, Misery, Or Mastery?

Those Who Talk

"Bounce" ideas off of another. Allow another to "talk back" to you. Again, it is crucial that you choose carefully the ones with whom you share your dream-ideas. Appropriate, well-targeted, and effective sharing should yield productive and profitable "talking" from those "in the know."

It is interesting to note that those "in the know" may actually prove to be persons from a mix that includes your competition, your family members, and your cheerleaders. Note afresh that there are exceptions to most every rule. You will often hear "effective," "helpful," and "authentic" talk coming from sources that equal your competition, your family members, and your cheerleaders. Remember our recurring mastery-theme here: "Let discernment be your guide."

Tape The Talk

You will be wise to tape, with the knowledge of your encouragers, their comments. The recording can be short and selective. Or you may prefer to record the entire session. An overwhelming majority of us make it a habit not to record those who uniquely

THE KANGAROO FACTOR

inform and encourage us. We are missing a huge dream-mastery boat here.

Two of my ardent supporters are my father and my grandmother. The verb "are" rather than "were" is operative here because taped recordings enable me to continue benefiting from their words. (My father passed away at age 53 when I was 18; my grandmother passed away at age 103 when I was 43.) Granted, memory is a powerful gift. Its potency can be enhanced and expanded when you "tape the talk." Our moments are shortest at their longest, most delicate at their strongest. Do not waste the talk of your enthusiastic supporters. Tape it.

Your connections need not die through distance or death. They can live on, leading you toward dream-mastery, when you remember to tape the talk.

Those who talk to you about your dream can impact you and your dream immediately. If you are astute enough to tape the talk, then the benefit of that very single conversation may be multiplied as many times as you hear the talk you taped.

Those Who Listen

Not only do those who talk affect whether or not we master our dream, but those who listen can

Mystery, Misery, Or Mastery?

also impact both dream-journey and dream-destination. Those who listen to you can service your dream.

Thirty-plus years of study and observation have taught me that you and I possess a tremendous capacity to "self-start," "self-destruct," and "self-correct" in relationship to the mastery of our dream. Often, the miracle in relationship to all of this is the talk "we speak" – the talk "someone else merely hears." Those who listen to us talk about our dream contribute significantly to the mastering of our dream without saying a word. When a dreamer talks and another listens, a catalyst is created that can ignite significant dream-movement. In similar fashion, when a dreamer talks, and another listens, the dreamer can miraculously interpret the transparency of the listener. That transparency-interpretation serves as a magnificent rudder for future steps of total reversal, minor modification, or awesome acceleration.

Those Who Confront

It is both tempting and easy to fool yourself into believing that only those who affirm you care about you and your dream. This is certainly not always the case. Often, those persons who are willing to confront you in certain areas will prove to be those who care the most about you and your dream-success.

With that said, may I once again simply remind you of that which you already know full well: "Often, those who care the most are those who care enough to suggest modifications."

This is certainly not a call to badger yourself with a composite of confrontation that is being hurled your way from every possible angle. It is, however, an invitation to learn and profit in relationship to your specific dream from those who care enough to challenge you and your thoughts in certain areas. It will be helpful to remember at this point that mastery, as it relates to your dream, has everything in the world to do with developing a positive relationship with those who care enough to challenge you. Postpone no longer an appropriate need to meet with those who are willing to care enough to question your presuppositions and even your precious plans.

Those Who Have Written

Your dream-helpers list must include authors and editors. How better can you expand and update your base of support? Your arsenal of dream-assistance

Mystery, Misery, Or Mastery?

can certainly feature a plethora of authors and editors who have written about dreaming and achieving.

Fully aware of this reality, I have included a substantial Recommended Reading List at the book's end. Inclusion in this list does not equal endorsement of a particular concept. Once again, you must exercise your choice-voice. I do, however, want you to have what I refer to as a massive "dreamer's smorgasbord" from which to choose.

I also want you to have the opportunity to benefit from some of my research, especially if you do not have the time or the inclination to pursue it in its largest context. Therefore, I want to highlight three entries from the Recommended Reading List. I, in no way, want to slight the other entries. Specifically, I want to illustrate how a particular author or editor can function as your dream-helper. Bibliographical data on each entry will be included in the Recommended Reading List beginning on page 267.

THE KANGAROO FACTOR

All In One Room

How would you like to bring many of the world's greatest dreamers into a single room? How would you like to benefit from their insights?

Peter Krass, editor of *The Book Of Entrepreneur's Wisdom – Classic Writing By Legendary Entrepreneurs*, has brought these great dreamers into one room, or one book. Your potential for benefiting from the powerful writings of these entrepreneurs is awesome. I wish there had been a book precisely like this decades ago.

I feel it inappropriate to list the names of all of those persons who are featured in this marvelous book. It will be helpful, however, for you to appreciate the scope of this massive assortment of dreamers. Therefore, I will list a significant number of those whose writings are shared. I encourage you to sample enough of the smorgasbord offerings so as to experience the fullness that they might bring to your dream.

The Book of Entrepreneur's Wisdom – Classic Writing By Legendary Entrepreneurs, as edited by Peter Krass, features an impressive cast of diverse dreamers and achievers including:

Mystery, Misery, Or Mastery?

Lillian Vernon
Harvey S. Firestone
Walley Amos
Barry Diller
Warren Avis
Andrew Carnegie
Conrad Hilton
Dave Thomas
J.C. Penney

Michael S. Dell
Benjamin Franklin
Clarence Birdseye
P.T. Barnum
Colonel Harland Sanders
Samuel Goldwyn
Henry Ford
Victor Kiam
Marquis M. Converse

Benefit from this book. It will make it possible for you to bring these effective dreamers into the same book-room with you.

From All Over The World

It is often my pleasure to deliver the baccalaureate message to graduating seniors. On occasion, the message gifts me with the opportunity to meet the valedictorian, the salutatorian, and the senior class president. In other instances, I benefit from reading about those who lead their class academically (valedictorian and salutatorian) and technically (class president).

My observation, based on what I have seen and what I have read, is worthy of notation. The

THE KANGAROO FACTOR

percentage of immigrants who have graduated at the top of their class, or near the top of their class, is remarkable. If you were to take the senior classes from throughout America and analyze them, you would discover that a number of these classes have elected class presidents who came to America from another country.

One could argue that these persons, coming to America from all over the world, have the odds stacked against them. In many instances they must learn a second language and absorb a new culture, even as they work before and after school. People like me, persons who struggle with dream-mastery, can learn a great deal from people like them, their parents, and their grandparents.

With this "from all over the world" theme as our current backdrop, it is now my pleasure to lift up for your consideration a book by a fellow speaker and author. Marcia Steele's *Making It In America – What Immigrants Know and Americans Have Forgotten* touches the issue that I am addressing here.

Her book affirms all Americans who dare to pursue dream-mastery. It is loaded with help for you and your dream. Her work equals what I would describe as a candid and personal guide for all dreamers. In *Making It In America*, Marcia A. Steele

Mystery, Misery, Or Mastery?

writes: "One of the biggest challenges facing us in America today is not global competition or technology, but rather complacency and fear! Half of us are complacent with the status quo and the other half live in fear of losing the status quo."

This dream-helper's book is loaded with numerous examples of immigrants from different nations and different walks of life who have experienced dream-mastery. It can certainly "fire your imagination."

From A Life Of Business To The Business Of Life

The preceding sub-heading is actually the sub-title for the book I now highlight. The lead title for this work is *Kiss Yourself Hello!* It challenges each dreamer to add "salt 'n pepper" to their lives in spite of their age.

When I challenge you to ponder this particular book, I recognize that I am certainly not alone. Those persons who have written favorably about Phil Parker's *Kiss Yourself Hello!* include: Les Brown, Fran Tarkenton, Nido R. Qubein, and Raleigh Pinskey.

THE KANGAROO FACTOR

Gift yourself with a copy of *Kiss Yourself Hello! From A Life Of Business To The Business Of Life* by Phil Parker. Allow Phil's insight to assist you as you sojourn toward dream-mastery. Benefit from Phil as he challenges you to: "Re-visit your past, study the present, build your dreams, and create your future."

Brain Food

Before we proceed, let me encourage you to think of a book as dream food, brain food, seizing food. If you cooperate with it, the appropriate book can enable you to leap from your pouch of postponement and land in the world of planned dreams and realized dreams.

The preceding sentence holds within it two crucial words to our thinking: "cooperate" and "appropriate." Be very selective in both your thinking and in your acting. Choose to read books that are appropriate to your internal mandates. When the appropriateness (integrity) test is passed, then cooperate with the portions of the book that authentically and effectively support your personhood. Be very careful here. The books you choose to read may well affect you and your dream!

Mystery, Misery, Or Mastery?

Ultimately, the food you feed your brain reveals its potency and make-up within the very core of your dreams!

Let There Be No Mystery

By now, there should be no doubt. Perpetual mystery is not worth your effort. Misery certainly does not merit your determination. That leaves mastery. Mastery wipes out mystery, misery, and mediocrity. Mastery demands and rewards your discipline.

Gift yourself with a discipline – a discipline that equals mastery. Let there be no doubt about your commitment to learning the art of mastery. Commit to being professional, process-focused, plan-centered, preparation-grounded, prophetic, positive, and personal. Commit to practicing and reaching. Commit to avoiding "dream-hinderers." Commit to benefiting from "dream-helpers." Commit to profiting from those who talk, those who listen, those who care enough to confront, and those who have written!

Let there be no mystery about it. Commitment is a thoroughfare toward dream-mastery!

Part Five

Celebrate The Cycle

CHAPTER 13

A Higher Consciousness

You probably remember it. It was that time when most cars and trucks had their brake lights positioned in the tail light area. Many years ago, it was determined that these brake lights would be more effective if they were supported by another brake light positioned just above the back seat, at the base of the rear window glass. By elevating this brake light, thus enhancing its visibility, lives would be saved. There was merit in the thinking.

At this writing, it is not unusual to notice vehicles that have this brake light not at the base of the

THE KANGAROO FACTOR

glass adjacent to the back seat – but higher still. This brake light is located considerably above the back seat and just below the roofline. As the extra brake light has been increasingly raised to a higher consciousness, visibility has increased even more. Safety has been enhanced even more.

Here, Here

That is precisely what I want to do with the remaining portions of *The Kangaroo Factor – Dream Big! Think Big! Seize The Moment!*. I hope to bring the very essence of this book to a higher consciousness for you, here and now. I hope to lay out afresh the very systems and cycles for you, here and now. I trust that you will respond to this higher consciousness, this higher visibility, by indeed dreaming big, thinking big, and seizing your moments of opportunity.

How will I do this? How will I raise the essence of our time together to a higher consciousness? I plan to increase the visibility of our system-concepts, to enhance their aliveness for you, through four tools:

- This Very Chapter
- The Mastery Of Discipline Poem

A Higher Consciousness

- A Treasury Of Power Points
- The Recommended Reading List

Concentrating Leads To A Higher Consciousness

If memory serves me correctly, there used to be a television game-show called "Concentration." For one reason or another, I have not seen it around in quite a while.

This is no time for your concentration to go away. In fact, this is the time for the very moments of your life to become more intensely informed and influenced by your concentration. To a large degree, your very dream-joy may depend upon it.

As you concentrate on the very heart of this book, as you bear down, as you swallow in, your dream-consciousness will increase. As you breathe every invigorating breath this book offers you, your dream-consciousness will be taken to a higher level. As you forge your own systems, you will discover something very exciting. As you consistently build and apply your own discipline of mastery, as you take responsibility for your own power to choose, you will discover the miracle of cycle.

THE KANGAROO FACTOR

You Have Not Lived All Of Your Life – Yet

The mistake became a lesson. The lesson became a teacher. I remain the beneficiary of my mistake.

The taxi left the airport in routine fashion. There had been little conversation between the driver and me. I sought to break the ice. I began with a question.

"Have you lived here all of your life?"

"No, not all of my life. I have not lived all of my life – yet."

My apology was quick to follow.

"I am sorry. I misspoke. I should have asked you if you have been living here all of your life – up to this point."

Birth your dream. Plan it. Do not postpone it. Pursue and nurture it.

Wherever your "here" is, you must remind yourself that you have only been living "here" up to this point. There is still time to dream big, still time to think big, still time to seize your moments. You

A Higher Consciousness

have not lived "here" all of your life – yet! "Pursuit" can switch places with "postponement" now.

You can experience both a higher dream-consciousness and the miracle of cycle now. You have not nearly lived all of your life – yet. A huge door may be opening for you right now. What are you going to do with it? Will it take you "somewhere" or "nowhere"? Will it equal "mystery" or "miracle"?

> **CONCENTRATION leads to a higher consciousness.
> A HIGHER CONSCIOUSNESS
> leads to the miracle of cycle.**

The Miracle Of Cycle

The process can be progressive, even though it is interrupted. The happening can begin again, even though it has just ended. The event is highly contagious, even though it is contained within you. The "it cannot get any better than this" just did. The "I cannot take it any higher" just happened. The cycle that was to end just started all over again. The crucible of dread yielded to dream, then to cycle, then to celebration, then to another cycle!

THE KANGAROO FACTOR

You discarded your postponement-pouch. A city was chosen. That led to a named dream and an awakened dream. That led to a giving in to joy. Then you targeted your thoughts. You invaded your own thought-life. You thought about the very thoughts you think. That led you to throw some thoughts in the dump, to take other thoughts to the bank. You viewed your dream-building as full of opportunity, not empty. You answered your "mystery, misery, or mastery" question. You gifted yourself with a "reach advantage." You enjoyed both the leaping and the landing. And it all felt good. It felt good because you knew it could actually start all over again. It could be forever defined by a perpetually changing higher consciousness.

Then you ran to him or to her, or maybe to them. Perhaps you hurried to be alone with Him. You just could not figure it out: "Which feeling was the strongest? Was it celebration or anticipation?" Then it grabbed you. You did not have to figure it out. At least for the moment, you could just let the joy be. And the miracle of cycle would start again soon enough!

CHAPTER 14

The Discipline Of Mastery

An enigma it is – this discipline of mastery.
You leave the pouch you hated so
Only to want it back – and soon.
Then you leave it for good.

And leap and land, and leap again.
You think you've mastered this,
This leaping stuff – far and high.
You think you surely have it down.

THE KANGAROO FACTOR

You see that's not the way it is.
For once growth seems to arrive,
You see there's more to do
And even much more to be.

So you become fueled to strive.
To strive, undeterred by this and that,
To hold to plan with firm of hand,
To experience fight, then fun, never flight.

To commence afresh – to leap again,
Just when you think you are done with that.
To see and craft and sculpt and mold,
To chisel from stone the dream you own.

To smile from head and heart's deep,
And taste it all so sweet.
To wonder at that which you hold,
And hope it will repeat.

~ Stephen M. Gower
Winter of 2000

**The leaping and the landing
require the DISCIPLINE.**

CHAPTER 15

A Treasury Of Power Points

Understanding that there will be moments when you will appreciate A Ready-Reference of Power Points, I have prepared for you a composite of the Power Points appearing in *The Kangaroo Factor*. They will be presented in book sequence, enabling you to visit afresh the particular concepts they capsule.

253

THE KANGAROO FACTOR

Introduction: Eight Rules To Dream By

- DEFINE your dream. SEE your dream happening! EXCITE and IGNITE. ENJOY and EXPECT. SEIZE your opportunities. MONITOR your thoughts. BRING home the dream. CELEBRATE the cycle.

Chapter One: Where Do You Want To Live?

- There is but one person who can ultimately take responsibility for your attitudes and behaviors. YOU are that person!

- How you choose to respond to your GIVEN and how you choose to GATHER determine your GROWTH. The GIVEN plus the GATHERED equals GROWTH.

- The glue that holds all of this together, or the fire that burns it all apart, equals the very CHOICES we make.

A Treasury Of Power Points

- Many of us do not see our dreams HAPPENING. We see our dreams NOT HAPPENING.

Chapter Two: Why Would You Want To Live In Could City?

- Could City is a DARK city. There are no excitement-lights, no accomplishment-lights, and no joy-lights!

Chapter Three: Have You Thought About Do City?

- Go where you have never gone before and LOVE it!
- You have every right to be EXCITED about being in Do City.

Chapter Four: Give Your Dream A Name

- The high dream that can call, caress, and challenge you has much to GIVE to you: place, power, purpose, poise, and passion.

THE KANGAROO FACTOR

- Your dreams also DEMAND much of you: your intelligence, your ingenuity, your inertia, your integrity. You should not fret, because you already have what it takes!

- Ask yourself, "Will this dream HELP me to go to bed most nights with satisfaction, and wake up most mornings with excitement?"

Chapter Five: Give Your Dream A Wake-Up Call

- "Go" will overpower "woe" when you take RESPONSIBILITY for your choosing power and stop blaming your struggle on "them" and "it."

- When you give in to joy, when you dream big, think big, and seize your moments, "woe" will take backseat to "GO."

Chapter Six: Give In To Joy

- The "submission-hold" need not reign superior. You and I do not have to give in to

A Treasury Of Power Points

despair. There is ANOTHER OPTION. It equals a confident "leaping and landing."

- Joy need not be confined to journey's end. To the contrary, journey's end is most quickly and easily reached when the very PURSUIT of the dream EQUALS JOY in and of itself.

- Stop putting all of your dream-eggs into a "one-moment" achievement-basket. Success equals not only the destination; it equals JOURNEY-STEPS as well.

- To give in to joy is to BALANCE your dream-journey with dream-satisfaction.

- Each of us needs to EXPERIENCE a huge "Yes," a resounding "Well Done," the validation of "Mission Accomplished."

- Ultimately, you do not find confidence. Confidence FINDS YOU as you pay the preparation price.

THE KANGAROO FACTOR

- Detours are not always dream-enemies. Detours may actually prove to be dream-friends because they may call you to DIFFERENTIATE.

- An effective dream-manager will DELEGATE a dream-step to one for whom the step-size is more appropriate.

- Differentiate between the little things that AGGRAVATE and the little things that ACTIVATE.

Chapter Seven: Think About The Thoughts You Think

- We must seize (LOCATE) our thoughts, set apart (ISOLATE) and examine our thoughts, and appropriately do something with (RELOCATE) our thoughts.

A Treasury Of Power Points

Chapter Eight: Tell Your Past Where To Go

- You will never dream your biggest dreams as long as your negative past-based thoughts DOMINATE your thinking.

- You will never dream your biggest dreams as long as you refuse to allow your positive, past-based thoughts to SERVE you.

- You can MINIMIZE, or ELIMINATE, the power of negative, past-based thoughts over you. You can ENHANCE, or EXPAND, the power of positive, past-based thoughts over you.

- To RELEASE or to RETAIN? That is the crucial issue.

- You do not have to stay the way you are. Past performance is definitely not indicative of future results! You possess the awesome POWER TO BECOME!

THE KANGAROO FACTOR

Chapter Nine: Throw Your Negative Thoughts In The Dump

- The THOUGHT-DUMPSITE can equal a VERY GOOD place.

- You are in charge of THOUGHT-CONSTRUCTION! You are in charge of THOUGHT-PLACEMENT!

- Remember something very crucial: "Ultimately, others will not determine how you feel about yourself unless you COOPERATE with them."

- It is much better to feel awkward about the EXCITING and the NEW than it is to feel awkward about the BORING, the MEANINGLESSNESS, and the STAGNATE.

- Your challenge is to be your BEST SELF, not THE HORRIBLE COMPOSITE of everyone else's best self.

- Your barometer is your BEST SELF, not your PERFECT SELF.

A Treasury Of Power Points

- There is ALWAYS ROOM for your negative thoughts in the dump!

Chapter Ten: Take Your Positive Thoughts To The Bank

- Your mind is a "MOLD AND HOLD" vessel.

- It is not enough to remove negative thoughts. Removed, negative thoughts must be replaced. If they are not removed and then replaced, negative thoughts will RESURFACE.

- The taking of your "keeper-thoughts" to the bank, so these thoughts can pay dividends of growth and achievement, is the SMART thing for you to do.

- You will FIND that the REMEMBERING can cause a remarkable growth, a remarkable discipline, and a remarkable giving in to joy.

THE KANGAROO FACTOR

Chapter Eleven: Empty Or Full?

- By now, you should feel like LEAPING – not for joy, but with joy!

- To see FULL, not empty, even when it might appear as empty as others, is to experience positive, give-in-to-joy thinking!

- You will grow and soar when you recognize and release what is already WITHIN you. There is a powerhouse arsenal within you that may have been DORMANT for decades.

- CAMOUFLAGE equals a move to get us thinking that the dream-purpose and dream-power is out there, not within us.

- The REMOVAL of the camouflage can be a springboard, a perpetual launching pad for the leaping.

- The STRATEGY plus the SKILLS equals the SOARING.

A Treasury Of Power Points

- A positive, purposeful, and profitable idea is a SOARING waiting to happen.

- Your self-talk determines whether you experience the discipline of MISERY (helpless, hurting) or the discipline of MASTERY (helpful, hopeful).

Chapter Twelve: Mystery, Misery, Or Mastery?

- PERPETUAL POSTPONEMENT will cloud your thinking if you repeatedly remain uncertain about the specifics of your dream

- A "NO-IDEA-WHICH-WAY-TO-GO" mentality is very dangerous. Mystery can certainly lead to something worse. It can lead to misery!

- No discipline may be more EFFECTIVE than self-discipline. No discipline may be more DIFFICULT than self-discipline.

THE KANGAROO FACTOR

- To MASTER your self-discipline is to reach your highest bar and then raise it.

- Mastery-arrival is always an ENIGMA. It never ends, yet it can always begin again. The practice process never finishes.

- Let all that is within you correspond with itself in such a professional way as to convince you that you are a person of INTEGRITY.

- Your "PLAN-IT" should be specific, monitorable, measurable, and close at hand.

- Joy rarely flies on wings named anything other than "PREPARATION."

- Be leery of THOUGHT EVAPORATION. Put your visualized dream-joy thoughts in writing.

- You will never be POSITIVE about your dream as long as you refuse to be PERSONAL about your dream.

A Treasury Of Power Points

- We are all special. One by one, we do have a SONG to sing, a DANCE to dance, a HEART to honor. Personalize your dream. Make your difference.

- SEPARATE those limits that can be modified and corrected from those limits about which you can do little.

- We should be so COMMITTED to big dreams, to big thinking, to moments seized and mastered, and to dream joy that we stop trying to sharpen claws we do not have.

- As it relates to limits and how they impact your dream, RECOGNIZE THE DIFFERENCE between discarding and modifying.

- You do not grow when you incessantly put yourself down. That is when you self-destruct. You GROW when you affirm yourself at the point of your strengths. That is when you SELF-CORRECT.

THE KANGAROO FACTOR

Chapter Thirteen: A Higher Consciousness

- CONCENTRATION leads to a higher consciousness. A HIGHER CONSCIOUSNESS leads to the miracle of cycle.

Chapter Fourteen: The Discipline Of Mastery

- The leaping and the landing require the DISCIPLINE.

Recommended Reading

Afterburn, Stephen. *Winning At Work Without Losing At Love.* Nashville: Thomas Nelson Publishers, 1994.

Arnot, Robert. *The Biology Of Success.* Boston: Little, Brown and Company, 2000.

Brown, Les. *Live Your Dreams.* New York: Avon Books, 1992.

Cameron, Ben. *The Big Picture: Getting Perspective On What's Really Important In Life.* Grand Rapids: Zondervan Publishing House, 1999.

Cameron, Julia. *The Vein Of Gold – A Journey To Your Creative Heart.* New York: Putnam, 1996.

Cathcart, Jim. *The Acorn Principle – Know Yourself – Grow Yourself.* New York: St. Martin's Press, 1998.

Cathy, S. Truett. *It's Easier To Succeed Than To Fail.* Nashville: Oliver Nelson, 1989.

Change, Richard. *The Passion Plan – A Step-By-Step Guide To Discovering, Developing, and Living Your Passion.* San Francisco: Jossey-Bass Publishers, 2000.

Covey, Stephen. *The Seven Habits Of Highly Effective People.* New York: Simon & Schuster, 1989.

THE KANGAROO FACTOR

Emerson, Ralph Waldo. *Self-Reliance And Other Essays.* United States: Barnes & Noble, 1995.

Geib, Michael J. *How To Think Like Leonardo De Vinci – Seven Steps To Genius Everyday.* New York: Dell Trade Paperback, 1998.

Gower, Stephen M. *The Focus Crisis – Nurturing Focus Within A Culture Of Change.* Toccoa: Lectern Publishing, 1996.

Gower, Stephen M. *Think Like A Giraffe – A Reach For The Sky Guide In Creativity And Maximum Performance.* Toccoa: Lectern Publishing, 1997.

Hartman, Amir and John Sifonis with John Cador. *Net Ready – Strategies For Success In The E-Conomy.* New York: McGraw-Hill, 2000.

Horn, Sam. *Cozentrate.* New York: Saint Martins Press, 2000.

Jolley, Willie. *It Only Takes A Minute To Change Your Life.* New York: St. Martin's Press, 1997.

Krass, Peter ed. *The Book Of Entrepreneur's Wisdom – Classic Writings By Legendary Entrepreneurs.* New York: John Wiley and Sons, Inc. , 1999.

Lewis, C.S. *Surprised By Joy.* New York: Bantam, 1986.

Mandino, Og. *Mission.* New York: Ballantine, 1986.

Recommended Reading List

Mandino, Og. *Secrets For And Happiness.* New York: Ballantine, 1995.

Maxwell, John C. *Failing Forward – Turning Mistakes Into Stepping Stones For Success.* Nashville: Thomas Nelson Publishers, 2000.

McGrath, Ellen. *The Complete Idiots Guide® To Beating The Blues.* New York: Alpha Books, 1998.

Parker, Phil. *Kiss Yourself Hello! From A Life Of Business To The Business of Life.* Atlanta: GOLDENeight Publishers, 1999.

Peale, Norman Vincent. *Imagining.* New York: Guideposts, 1982.

Peale, Norman Vincent. *The Power Of Positive Thinking.* New York: Fawcett, 1987.

Rohn, Jim. *The Seasons Of Life.* Irving: Jim Rohn International, 1996.

Rohn, Jim. *The Treasury Of Quotes.* Irving: Jim Rohn International, 1996.

Schwartz, David. *The Magic Of Thinking Big.* New York: Fireside, 1987.

Sherman, Doug and William Hendricks. *Your Work Matters To God.* Colorado Springs: NAVPRESS, 1998.

THE KANGAROO FACTOR

Shinn, Georgie. *The Miracle Of Motivation.* Illinois: Tyndale House, 1981.

Steele, Marcia. *Making It In America – What Immigrants Know And Americans Have Forgotten.* Atlanta: Maxmar, 2000.

Thoreau, Henry David. *Walden.* Philadelphia: Running Press, 1990.

Tullier, Michelle. *The Complete Idiots Guide® To Overcoming Procrastination.* Indianapolis: Alpha Books, 1999.

Von Oech, Roger. *A Kick In The Seat Of The Pants.* New York: Harper & Row Publishers, 1986.

Von Oech, Roger. *A Whack On The Side Of The Head.* New York: Warner Books, 1983.

Weylman, C. Richard. *Opening Closed Doors – Keys To Reaching Hard-To-Reach People.* Illinois: Irwin, 1994.

Wooden, John. *Wooden: A Lifetime Of Observations On And Off The Court.* Chicago: Contemporary Books, 1997.

Ziglar, Zig. *Over The Top.* Nashville: Thomas Nelson Publishers, 1994.

About The Author

Stephen M. Gower, Certified Speaking Professional, works with organizations who want a fresh approach to leading change and with individuals who want to focus on professional growth. He is considered one of the country's most powerful speakers.

He has given more than 4,000 presentations and is a best selling author of twelve books. Mr. Gower holds a Bachelors Degree from Mercer University and a Masters Degree from Emory University.

The Gower Group, Inc.
P.O. Box 714
Toccoa, Georgia 30577
1-800-242-7404
www.stephengower.com
smg@stephengower.com